A Touch of Class

A Touch of Class

THE FRANK MYLER STORY

Maurice Bamford

VERTICAL EDITIONS

www.verticaleditions.com

First published in the United Kingdom in 2010 by
Vertical Editions, Unit 4a, Snaygill Industrial Estate,
Skipton, North Yorkshire BD23 2QR

www.verticaleditions.com

ISBN 978-1-904091-39-4

A CIP catalogue record for this book is available from the
British Library

The author would like to thank Robert Gate for his help
with information and photos used in this book

Cover design and typeset by HBA, York

Printed and bound by Cromwell Press Group,
Trowbridge

CONTENTS

With thanks to Frank Myler for allowing me to tell his story and for helping with many of the details.

Maurice Bamford

ACKNOWLEDGEMENTS

The subject of this biography, Frank Myler, did so much in his long and distinguished career it would have been virtually impossible to have completed the book alone. To help me achieve my goal I was lucky enough to call on the services of two great rugby league historians, Raymond Fletcher and Robert Gate. Both helped immensely.

Frank himself set the ball rolling with tales of his early days at Widnes and his experiences of three tours of Australia and New Zealand, with snippets of his international career taken from Robert Gates' wonderful book *Rugby League Lions: 100 Years of Test Matches*. Also I had super help from Frank's cousin, Tony Karalius, one of my old mates from my Central Park days. An excellent and lifelong golfer, Frank made a really great subject to write about and how could his story be anything other than fantastic with the main man being the last touring captain, to date, to lift the Ashes Cup in Sydney back in 1970. A big thanks to all who contributed.

INTRODUCTION

My intention was always to write about as many great rugby league players as possible but stories do not come any bigger than this biography of Frank Myler, international, county and club player, international and club coach and avid worker for the Widnes club as secretary. Frank is special to his own, as well as the current, generation of rugby league players as the last Great Britain captain to lift the Ashes Cup after beating Australia in their own country on the 1970 tour. Fourteen years later Frank was chosen to lead the Great Britain Lions tourists back to Australia and New Zealand as coach of that tour.

Frank's other sporting love is golf. A very good player, he acted as a caddy from being a young boy and learned the practices of top golfers at an early age. A very likable man with a pleasant, approachable manner, Frank has that special gift as a player and coach to instil belief in his team mates and squads. An unassuming man, Frank would no doubt be embarrassed by any sort of unearned bouquets from me, except it is a fact of life that Frank is one of the most admired former players and coaches in the game to this day.

Frank's early reputation was made as a strong running, exceptional footballer at stand off half for the Widnes club. In international and county football Frank's ability to make play for others combined with his own strong finishing also allowed him to operate as a terrific centre three quarter. He is above all a Widnes lad! His cool head in a crisis held him in good stead throughout his rugby league career and his pedigree in the game is of the highest quality. Frank's first cousins are the famous Karalius family, possibly the two most famous of the Karalius brothers were Vincent and Tony. Vincent was the great international loose forward of St Helens and Widnes whilst Tony, Vincent's younger brother, was an excellent player and an international hooker for various clubs notably St Helens and Fulham.

The Myler side of the family also produced some excellent players over a long period including two top class international players and several who were very near that level. A close knit family, the Myler and Karalius families lived close and grew up together in the tough Widnes town in the austere immediate post war years. Another bond was the staunch religious upbringing the two families shared in that strong Catholic neighbourhood.

The humour of that upbringing was also special. Widnes folk possess a natural, likeable persona. Humour plays a huge part in the lives of the hard working people near the river Mersey. Even now, Frank, in his quiet way, has his company in stitches with tales of things that happened to him on the field of play. He will laugh at the funny side of the game but never knock any former team mate or opponent. His type of humour shines through when he relates the tale of playing with the big, hard as nails, comical late forward Frank Collier at Widnes. Frank and the late Ray Owen operated at half back and had a move which sent Frank attacking down the blind side of a scrum. Frank Collier had taken some free golf balls from Frank Myler, as he had connections in the golfing game and was given free balls every now and then. Frank Collier was then transferred to Salford and knew of the blind side move between Frank and Ray. An early scrum in the game between Salford and Widnes allowed Ray to send Frank charging down the short side. Frank Collier shot out of the Salford second row and stopped Frank Myler with a bell ringer of a stiff arm tackle, picked up the stand off and back slammed him followed by the 17 stone bulk of Collier with the elbow in the sternum for good measure! Frank was 'cleaned out' but bravely regained his feet and with a big effort played the ball back to the dummy half. As Frank staggered away, big Frank Collier put his arm around Frank and whispered, 'Can you get me some more golf balls Frank?' This epitomises the humour in our great game in those days. It was physical and sometimes downright brutal but they were great days never the less.

Currently Frank still enjoys his golf at the Widnes Golf Club and although his rugby playing days are long behind him, Frank is always happy to discuss the modern game and style of play at length and has some very interesting theories about it. When you read about Frank Myler's playing exploits in *A Touch of Class* it is obvious that he is a total gentleman and one of the game's most admired former players.

1

GROWING UP IN WIDNES AND SIGNING FOR THE CLUB

The area named Newtown in South Widnes was where Frank Myler was born on 4 December 1938. His mam and dad, Annie and John [Jack] Myler, raised a family of five sons and one daughter, Doreen. The sons were named Gerald, Anthony [Tony], Edward [Ted], Francis [Frank] and Michael. Shortly after Frank was born the family moved to a new scheme of council housing in Lowerhouse Lane, about 200 yards from Naughton Park, the home of Widnes RLFC.

At that time war clouds were beginning to form in Europe and in September 1939, Britain entered into the battle as the Second World War began. Widnes was a crucial chemical refining and production area, vital to the country's war effort. Jack Myler worked in the chemical industry and his wife, Annie, went to work in the ammunition factory. The chemical workers of Widnes worked long hours to support the war effort and Jack Myler was working 12 hour shifts throughout the war. Widnes was a regular target for the enemy bombers who hoped to destroy the vital chemical works as well as the area's links to the great seaport of Liverpool whose docks were a prime target.

When Frank was a youngster, the area of modern houses where he lives now was fields. In March 1941 a German bomber was shot down and crashed onto those fields. Although Frank was too young to remember this, he remembers hearing stories of the event. The plane passed very low over the Myler house and the deafening noise frightened everyone in the neighbourhood. The plane had been shot down by anti-aircraft guns and came down in a field about 300 yards from Frank's home. Two German airmen, the pilot and a crew member, were killed in the crash but three other airmen bailed out. They were captured later and taken to the local police station where they were interrogated by the RAF Intelligence Service. The two dead airmen were buried in the local cemetery but were repatriated to Germany many years later. Frank says, 'Although I was far too young to have any memories of this incident, the story of the crash became legendary amongst us kids and we regularly searched the field for mementos. Obviously, by this time all evidence of the crashed plane had been removed, but we often found other things from the war like pieces of shrapnel and spent bullets.'

Frank loved golf from a young age and, in fact, was involved with golf well before he became a rugby league player. He began caddying at eight years old for 9d (in old money, equivalent to less than 5p nowadays) per nine holes. He tells a story about when he used to caddy for two gentlemen who played every Sunday morning at 9 a.m. Frank went to early mass on Sundays so he didn't miss out on his caddying business. Playing off the first tee, the drive had to clear a ditch onto the green and regular as clockwork these two elderly gentlemen, who always played with brand new balls, dropped their first shots into the ditch. Frank used to jump into the ditch, stand on the balls, mark where they were and then retrieve them later to sell on. After a few months of this happening, one of the gentlemen said to Frank, 'We seem to be losing a lot of new balls, Frank. Why's that do you think?' Frank had to think quickly.

'Well there are always lots of kids from the estate in that ditch, looking for golf balls. They might be stealing the balls!'

The experienced gentleman then suggested that Frank should stand in the ditch until they were on the green and therefore could warn off any kids taking a fancy to the brand new balls. Frank was kicking himself because now he had lost his 'new balls sales'. He thought, 'Why didn't I keep my mouth shut?'

Frank's schooling began at St Bede's Infant School which was near to his home. He then made the natural progression to St Bede's Junior School where his teacher, Mr Appleton, introduced him to his first organised game of rugby league. Mr Appleton was responsible for cultivating the nine year old Frank's interest in sport. Frank says, 'He instilled into his pupils a belief that playing a team game like rugby league was not only adding a sporting string to our bow but that the game was a great character builder too'. St Bede's School did not have any playing fields or outside recreational area, apart from the school yard, so the young boys had to walk some distance to a field behind the local Territorial Army Barracks in Peelhouse Lane to play their rugby. Frank was soon chosen for the St Bede's under 11's team which played in inter-schools competitions. These matches were usually played on Leigh Recreational Ground and St Bede's were a hard team to beat. They won all before them.

Away from school, Frank and the other youngsters living on the new Lowerhouse housing estate were fortunate to have a large grassed area in the centre of the scheme. This meant they had somewhere to kick a ball around. Being close to Naughton Park meant that rugby league was a favourite game. Indeed, most male Widnesians had an interest in the sport either through active participation in local amateur teams or as spectators. Frank's dad, Jack, played rugby league at school but like most of the men of that era, when they left school, work and family responsibilities took over. It is interesting to note that the area within a half mile radius of Naughton Park, the Widnes ground, was a fertile breeding ground for rugby league talent. Many of the young lads who kicked a ball around on the fields near Lowerhouse Lane were destined to wear the jersey of Widnes RLFC and other prestigious rugby teams in later years. This small area produced three Australian Tour captains from the neighbouring housing estates who went on to represent their country at international level. Among those lads from the neighbouring housing estates who went on to play professionally were Eric Bate and his brother Ronnie, John Broome, Tom Brophy, Harry Dawson, brothers Dennis, Tony and Vince Karalius, George Kemel, Dougie Laughton, Alan Prescott, Horace Shaw and Tom Smith.

When he was 13 years of age, Frank left St Bede's Junior School and moved on to Sts John Fisher and Thomas More Secondary Modern School, or simply 'Fisher and More' as it is known locally.

Frank says he was fortunate here to have had the benefit of 'two exceptional rugby league coaches'. They were his teachers Peter Walsh and Peter Quinn. Whilst Mr Appleton at St Bede's taught him the rudiments of the sport and inspired an interest in the game, at Fisher and More School Mr Walsh and Mr Quinn taught him about passing the ball, not carrying it too far, how to work as a member of a team and plan your moves.

Big for a schoolboy, Frank's natural position appeared to be at loose forward. He was selected and played for Lancashire Schoolboys in the second row. He says, 'I was a biggish lad and loved the freedom of playing second row. I found that I didn't have to rely on my size alone as I had a natural bit of pace, not electrifying but enough to get by on and was light enough on my feet to beat a player with a step or with a dummy, swerve or change of pace'.

But Frank was still only 14 years old and the earliest one could be signed on as a professional player was at 16. Several of his schoolboy rugby league playing mates had, on leaving school at 15, joined a junior side at St Patrick's Catholic club and played at under 16 level. St Pats had a very good side with three or four former Lancashire schoolboy players in the team. Playing at loose forward, Frank was outstanding. He was a good, natural footballer with good hands, decent pace and a sound, hard tackler.

When Frank left school he followed his dad into the chemical trade. Jack Myler didn't want Frank to work in that environment, but there was little work elsewhere in the Widnes area as most factories manufactured chemicals. The firm Frank worked for was called W.J. Bush Ltd and a well known top amateur player, Jack Nolan worked at the same firm. Jack Nolan played in Open Age Rugby League and on leaving work one Friday tea time, he button holed Frank to ask him if he fancied a game with his team who were going to be a man short because of injury. Jack said, 'If you play Frank, it won't be at loose forward. I'd like you to play stand off! We play Crosfields at Warrington'.

Frank agreed to play and duly travelled with this new team to Crosfields. What Jack failed to mention was that the game was against a top Open Age side and Crosfields had several ex professional players in their side, all big, strong men. The two packs seemed immense compared to the forwards Frank was used to playing with and the backs were all biggish men with bags of experience. Frank's team had one or two players with professional experience at Widnes, so he was in good company. Once over the shock of changing position to stand off half, as well as the culture shock of playing against men for the first time, Frank settled down to enjoy the game. His natural ability began to show through as his personal confidence took control. He ended up having an excellent game.

After the match, a bloke approached Frank and asked his name, 'Frank Myler,' he replied.

The man looked at Frank and said, 'Oh yes, I saw you play for Lancashire Schoolboys last season but you were at loose forward then. Look Frank, I'd like you to come across to Wilderspool and train with Warrington and meet our coach, Ces Mountford.' Frank knew of Ces Mountford, a New Zealander and one of the finest stand off halves of his day for Wigan.

Frank talked it over with his Dad, who was a little worried about the travelling to and from Warrington in winter time. But the pair went across to meet Ces Mountford who made it plain that Warrington wanted the young Frank Myler to join them. 'I was impressed with Ces Mountford. He seemed a genuine bloke and had a nice relaxed attitude. He was honest and told me that he had not seen me play but that he trusted the ability of his chief scout who was adamant that Warrington should sign me. Ces Mountford described the workings of the Wilderspool club, made an offer of a signing on fee, talked about how playing with a good squad of players would help with my development as a player and, to his credit, advised me to think about all he had told us. He said I should consider his offer for a few days then let him know how I felt,' Frank explained.

Warrington had a hugely successful team at the time, and as well as the travelling there was also the point about Frank's position as a loose forward and his chances of breaking into that terrific pack that Ces Mountford had put together. Frank still considered himself a loose forward so there were many discussions to take place before making a decision. Remember, Frank was only 15 years of age. He decided to thank Warrington for their interest in his future but he wanted to play for Widnes, his hometown club, as it had always been an ambition of his.

In the meantime other professional clubs were showing an interest in this talented youngster who was by now almost 16 and of a signing on age. That grand small town club, Leigh, contacted Frank with an offer of £250 to sign for them and there was a certain amount of interest from his cousin Vince Karalius's club, the great St Helens. Although Frank had nailed his colours to the mast for Widnes, he heard nothing from the club about him signing on for them. This hurt Frank as two or three good clubs had shown an interest in him. He wondered if Widnes thought he had some defect in his play that turned them off signing him,

Then one evening Brendan Karalius, Frank's uncle 'Branner' (Vince's dad), visited Jack and Frank. When Frank mentions his Uncle Branner, he smiles with warm affection. A real character, Branner was the man the family turned to in cases of emergency, like the time when Jack and Annie's chimney was blocked. Jack went across to his brother in law and asked him to see if he could unblock the chimney! Branner arrived as Jack was on his way to work. 'I'll shift it for you Jack,' said Branner and went back home for his tools. He came back with a shotgun! Sticking the gun up the chimney, he let go with both barrels and this unblocked the chimney alright. It worked a treat but left a ton of soot in his sister's house! When Jack returned from work he nearly had a fit! But at least the chimney worked.

However, the reason for Branner's visit that particular evening was to see if Frank would be interested in going along to Knowsley Road, having a word with the coach and attending a Summer School on Tuesday and Thursday evenings at the ground. Branner was scouting for St Helens and was amazed that the Widnes club hadn't been in for Frank before this.

After going to Knowsley Road, Frank was as impressed with the great Jim Sullivan as he had been with the Warrington boss, Ces Mountford and he attended, and enjoyed, Summer School at Saints. It was easy to see that Ces Mountford had worked under Jim Sullivan for a few years as his attitude was very similar to the great Wigan full back. He was experienced, clear thinking, provided sound advice and appeared to be a nice, open gentleman.

Whilst training one evening at the Summer School there was a buzz that the chap walking up towards the Saints board room was the famous Welsh stand off, Cliff Morgan. He was expected to sign at St Helens and Jim Sullivan went across to shake hands with the rugby union kingpin. Later Cliff decided to stay in the union game.

By all accounts Saints wanted Frank as a loose forward. It is always difficult to know how much a young player will grow from 17 years of age onwards or what will be his best natural playing weight. Frank was almost 6 feet tall and athletically built as opposed to being bulky. Frank always said that if he had devoted as much time to weight training as his cousin Vince Karalius, then Frank and Vince may well have been a similar build. 'Vinty was a fanatical trainer. He used to pump weights, run mile after mile and exercise hour after hour. He was totally dedicated to building, as near as possible, the iron hard physique required to reach the top at loose forward in this hardest of team games,' he said.

Frank's individual training methods were to concentrate on sprinting over 30 yards. 'I had seen most of the top players at Widnes when we watched our local team. The loose forwards were all usually tallish with good physiques, like John Whiteley of Hull. The stand offs all had great acceleration as well as a football brain which planned what to do when they had gone clear. Their breaks normally ended with a pass to the supporting centres or a speedy loose forward,' Frank said. Speed off the mark and a fast moving 30 yards was what most stand offs dreamed of because if they got away with pace, hardly anyone would catch them over that 30 yards. 'I would sprint from standing starts, rolling starts and turning starts to give an edge to speed off the mark.'

When the young Frank Myler did move to stand off half, he soon picked up the importance of spotting a gap, calling for quick ball and hitting that gap hard. Frank explained, 'I played with, and against, some great players who could read a game. You would wait patiently, looking for a weakness in the opposing line, then, possibly in the play before, you would spot an opening and a quick, "Let's have it!" meant you wanted the ball, fast. A good pass and these great players would have you through the gap and away. If they carried the ball too far, say a couple of strides, then the gap would close but nine times out of 10 their timing of the pass was perfect. It was important to be able to act swiftly and accurately with your handling in those days and you relied on those key players to be aware of where the openings may come. If you were on the same wavelength, you all worked in unison. Alex Murphy, Vinty and, in my opinion, the unsung hero Kel Coslett, all had the gift of spotting early openings so when you wanted the quick ball on call you received it!'

Although Frank was still training at St Helens he hadn't yet played a trial for them. Then one Saturday afternoon he heard a whisper on the grapevine that Widnes were interested. The following morning two of the Widnes directors, Mr Stirrup and the legendary Alex Higgins, arrived at Frank's home with an offer to sign him. Before that, Saints had wanted Frank to play three trial games, Leigh had offered £250 up front and Warrington's Ces Mountford offered £200 and said, 'I've not seen you play son, but our scouts say you are worth that fee'. But Frank's heart was at Widnes, so he was delighted to sign at 16 years of age for a fee of £50 plus £25 after the first 12 team games.

After the visit of the two Widnes directors, Frank was told to report for his first training session the following Tuesday evening. Obviously the youngster, at 16, faced this prospect with a degree of trepidation but his fears were allayed on the Tuesday evening when his neighbour, Harry Dawson, knocked on the door to congratulate him. Harry Dawson's arrival was followed shortly afterwards by another neighbour, George Kemel, also wanting to wish him well. Both Harry Dawson and George Kemel were established members of the first team so as the three of them made their way to Naughton Park that evening Frank was boosted by the moral support. When they arrived at the ground, Frank parted company with Harry and George who were headed for the first team dressing room whilst Frank was bound for the 'A' team section. Any nerves were quickly dispelled as he was welcomed to the 'A' team dressing room by Mr Harold Foster, the bathman, who looked after the jerseys and general kit. As the dressing room quickly filled up Frank was made welcome by the other members of the team and before long he settled into his new role and new surroundings at

Widnes. Frank remembers that in those early days at Naughton Park he was helped enormously by some of the more established players like Tom Smith, Eric Bate and Lal Tomlinson who were always on hand to offer help and advice to the young player.

When he had signed on for Widnes Frank received his £50 signing on fee with an agreement that he would receive £25 after he had played 12 games. Later there was some problem with the club's interpretation of the deal. The first payment went through without a hitch and after Frank played 12 games, the club paid the promised £25 less tax! Frank questioned this but was told that it was taxed because it had been earned. 'No,' Frank insisted, 'this was part of my signing on fee.' The board did not agree and Frank was so incensed that he said he would not play again without the club first meeting the full signing on fee. Frank's dad went to Naughton Park to advise the secretary that he had never butted into Frank's decisions before, as Frank could speak for himself, but he felt he should warn them that if the club did not meet its promise over the signing on fee, he would not permit Frank to play again for the club. Common sense prevailed and the club paid.

When Frank signed at Widnes, the coaching staff were a joint affair with the great Tommy Shannon as first team coach and Frank Tobin as trainer. The 'A' team coach was a nice bloke and a former player, Bob Harper. Tommy Shannon was great for Frank. He helped Frank immensely, carefully adjusting his change from loose forward to stand off half. Tommy had been a terrific half back partner for many years with the equally great Tommy McCue at Widnes so he knew the art of the stand off half off by heart. Frank developed well and played only a handful of 'A' team games before making the first team as a regular.

One of the benefits of Frank's game was his adaptability. He could give a good account of himself if playing virtually anywhere in the backs. But he hated playing in the centre! Frank played in the centre for Great Britain and Lancashire County with great distinction, but disliked the position intensely. He loved the midfield freedom of stand off half where he had the option of creating for his centres or taking on the opposition himself and was not reliant on anything except his own ability. In the centre, players constantly hoped their team mates were doing their jobs correctly on both attack and defence. If they did not do the job then they could make centres look bad. Stand off players were their own boss! Tommy Shannon tailored Frank's game and smoothed off the rough edges. As a loose forward, Frank was on the small side in professional football and may well have had to bulk up for the job, but at stand off half he was on the big side meaning he was a strong stand off.

Talking to Frank about the wealth of stand offs around in his day, one might be amazed to hear that in the trials before the 1960 World Cup he was rated as sixth choice for that competition. The five stand offs in front of Frank were Dave Bolton [Wigan], Harry Archer [Workington Town], Alan Kellett [Oldham], Harold Poynton [Wakefield Trinity] and George Parkinson [Swinton]. Come trial day and four of them were injured so Frank played and scored three tries to land the position of stand off half for Great Britain in all the World Cup games.

Frank Myler signed for his home town club and served them well for 12 seasons. He made the transition from schoolboy loose forward to professional stand off half without a hitch showing his unique aptitude for the game as well as his ability to handle these challenging, sometimes traumatic, changes in position. His record speaks for itself: after only a few 'A' team games, Frank made his debut for the first team at the age of 17 years and 23 days when he ran out for Widnes at Naughton Park against physical Liverpool City on 27 December 1955. Frank scored two fine tries in his memorable debut and helped his team to an 18–2 win. The adventure that was to take Frank to a superb Wembley win as well as halfway around the world three times to Australia and New Zealand had begun.

2

MAKING HIS WAY
IN THE GAME

As was the way in those days, good youngsters were eased into big time football. Debuts were usually hand picked but only rarely was the young player subjected to the ultimate test, that of playing against the best teams in the land. So Frank's first game was against Liverpool City as mentioned, the day after Boxing Day. On New Year's Eve, Frank was in the first team again to play against Blackpool Borough away at the seaside! This time Widnes lost 20–12. The next game was on 14 January at Central Park, Wigan. The Widnes directors thought it prudent not to include Frank, a 17 year old prospect, in possibly one of the hardest games of the season. Roy Butler took Frank's place in the Widnes team—Frank had taken Roy's place in the Liverpool and Blackpool games. The Widnes team which beat Liverpool City was Colin Parker; Gordon Williamson, John Sale, Jimmy Andrews, Peter Ratcliffe; Frank Myler, Percy Davies; Tom Smith, Ted Hayes, Jim Royle, Dennis Tobin, Ernie Simpson and George Kemel. Against Blackpool the side was John Sale; Gordon Williamson, Lal Kinsey, Tom Galligan, Peter Ratcliffe; Frank Myler, Percy Davies; Ron Rowbottom, Ted Hayes, Edgar Bate, Jim Royle, Ernie Simpson and George Kemel.

Frank was back in the Widnes side the week after, when he figured at stand off against the ultra tough Oldham side at Naughton Park. This was another experience for young Frank as this Widnes v Oldham game, as expected, was a tight affair played out amongst the forwards. The victory went to Widnes by the narrowest of results, 11–10. Frank remembered that 'Those Oldham forwards were all big, sturdy men who were playing to win to their fullest extent: Ken Jackson, Jack

Keith, Charlie Winslade, Sid Little, Bryn Goldswain and strong running Alan Davies in the centre and the speedy Dick Cracknell and Terry O'Grady on the wings'. As a young stand off, he witnessed every aspect of the game at league level from a grandstand seat. Frank maintained his position at stand off half in all but one of that season's games—the game he didn't play in was the stiff trip to Station Road against Swinton where Widnes lost 15–2.

Frank recorded seven tries in his first 15 first team games in an excellent start to his career. But Widnes won only four of those 15 games. Granted there were some difficult games among these fixtures such as St Helens away, Halifax at home in the Challenge Cup first round, Barrow, Workington Town, Swinton and Rochdale Hornets all away, Wigan at home and Salford away. These were just some of the hard games in which Frank played in his early education into his chosen professional sport. 'I was learning about the game at the top level and loving every second of it. I watched how various backs beat their opposition and remembered what they'd done. Some used a step, some acceleration, some sheer pace and some played it extremely hard and tried to out face you with the hard stuff,' Frank recalled. The game against St Helens, away, for instance, showed just how strong the Saints team was then, with international players in most positions. The Saints team was Glyn Moses; Steve Llewellyn, Doug Greenall, Reg Senior, Frank Carlton; Bill Finnan, Austin Rhodes; Alan Prescott, Frank McCabe, Nat Silcock, George Parsons, Vince Karalius and Max Garbler.

Widnes's last win of the 1955–56 season was on Saturday 10 March when they beat Leigh 24–4 at Naughton Park. Frank scored a try against Leigh in this win as well as tries against Doncaster at home in the 30–10 win, the 14–5 defeat at Rochdale, the defeat at home to Salford 18–12 and the 19–18 away defeat at Blackpool Borough!

Some of the team names from those days may well catch the younger reader by surprise. Rochdale Hornets were a strong team at home, as were Liverpool City who for years signed good youngsters and transferred them on to much bigger clubs to manage their finances. Oldham were an incredibly hard side to beat, either home or away, as were Hunslet who took no prisoners at their tight Parkside ground. As the Widnes club progressed and some of its younger stars proceeded in their careers, their results improved and Widnes began to reclaim the high reputation they held during the twenties and thirties. Frank played every game with an enthusiasm that his first team games were giving him, and he was learning all the time. His first season in top class rugby league read Widnes played 39, won 14, lost 25, drawn 0. Frank's record that first season was played 15, won 4, lost 11 drawn 0. The Widnes board realised they had bought a diamond of a young player.

Widnes were searching for a regular squad around this time. Frank looked to be the answer to the stand off position but he was only very young. Players who gained selection at stand off half prior to Frank's arrival were Jimmy Andrews, Roy Butler, Roy Charles and Lal Kinsey. Frank's regular partner at scrum half was Percy Davies and the other member of the triangle at loose forward was George Kemel who went on later to be the regular hooker for Widnes.

There were very few 'easy' games in the league programme in those days but Frank was progressing nicely and scoring some good tries as he acquired vital experience needed to make his mark in professional rugby league. The only way to help Frank up the ladder was to play him regularly in one position. The list of established international stand offs at the time Frank was beginning his career was daunting for a youngster. These internationals included Ray Price at Warrington, Dave Bolton at Wigan and Harry Archer at Workington and all three vied for the one position, with Harold Poynton of Wakefield Trinity also there or thereabouts. Frank and Tom Smith, the big front row forward, were good mates. Tom went on in later years to become Chairman of the club. Another great servant of the club, Harry Dawson, was playing at that time in the centre for Widnes.

So Frank's first season in professional rugby ended. He had every reason to be pleased with his introduction to the game and to the crucial stand off half role he enjoyed. There were some very good judges of footballers at Widnes and all were delighted at the progress made by this young, strong, skilful and alert stand off.

Frank's first full season, 1956–57 began with a trip to St Helens. In those days Widnes seemed to meet Saints regularly in the first game of the season. The result of this game was a resounding 29–0 defeat for Widnes. On that opening day Widnes chose to field John Sale; Gordon Williamson, Billy Wright, Tom Galligan, Peter Ratcliffe: Frank Myler, Percy Davies; Tom Smith, Gordon Murray, Harold Tomlinson, Vinny Smith, Harry Lamb and Dennis Tobin. The St Helens team was Glyn Moses; Steve Llewellyn, Doug Greenall, Brian Howard, Frank Carlton; John 'Todder' Dickinson, Austin Rhodes; Alan Prescott, Len McIntyre, Nat Silcock, George Parsons, Walter Delves and Vince Karalius.

A win against Dewsbury 29–4, in which Frank scored a try, was followed by two home defeats against Workington Town 13–6 and Barrow 17–7 in the Lancashire Cup. Widnes next played at Central Park against Wigan in a match that Frank missed. But he was back in the centre a week later against Whitehaven at Naughton Park. They lost this game 17–12 and Frank didn't play the next six games before returning at stand off half in the 18–11 win away at Castleford.

For most young players who arrive and show good form and class, there is, inevitably, a period when things go a wee bit wrong and the youngster needs to assess things to get his game back on track. This happened to Frank too. From his return on 27 October, Frank played in seven consecutive games, of which the team won four. Then a bad defeat at Mount Pleasant, Batley was followed by four straight defeats to St Helens, Oldham and Barrow at home and Halifax at Thrum Hall. Frank played in two of these defeats, Oldham and Barrow. Frank returned for the Batley game at Widnes and the team recorded an 11–4 win. After another three weeks out, Frank made a superb return at stand off for the 8–6 home win over Warrington where he had an outstanding game. Frank did not play at all in the final seven games of this season due to torn ankle ligaments. In total he played 20 games in this season and missed 22.

It was a huge contrast the following season when Frank played in all but one of Widnes's games and scored 22 tries in the season. Obviously he had been handled correctly by the coaches at Naughton Park, and the club were about to see the best of this young man. Gradually the future international stand off half-centre was learning his trade at professional level, and would go on to great things as both player and captain of the Great Britain set up. But there is much to come in his league career before that.

3

SETTLING INTO REGULAR FIRST TEAM RUGBY LEAGUE

The 1957–58 season was possibly the most important one in Frank's apprenticeship at stand off half. In this season Frank played in 40 of the club's 41 games all at stand off half. He also recorded 22 tries. The only game Frank missed was the 42–5 defeat at Workington Town where Lal Kinsey played at number 6 for the injured Frank Myler. Still only 19 years old, Frank displayed a strength and determination to mark him out as one of the brightest prospects in the league. His 22 tries were the product of fine support play, having a keen eye for an opening, and having the strength and pace to finish off with a try if given the chance.

In an acceptable season in which Frank played 40, won 23, lost 16, drawn 1, one of the highlights was the win at Naughton Park against a strong Barrow side that had beaten Widnes in Barrow 24–10 in the early season. The game in Widnes ended in a 31–8 home win in which Frank scored two tries. Other try scorers were Ray Owen (2), Harry Dawson, John Broome and Frank's cousin Eddie Myler. Harry Dawson kicked five goals. Eight days later, Frank recorded a hat trick of tries in the 31–7 win away to Doncaster. Widnes were beaten at Headingley 18–8 by Leeds in the league game in mid September but in the return game in early December at Naughton Park, Widnes pulled off a great 21–3 victory. The team that day for Widnes was Billy Wright; Peter Ratcliffe, John Broome, Harry Dawson, Gordon Williamson; Frank Myler, John Smith; Tom Smith, George Kemel,

Edgar Bate, Ken Hill, Derek Smith and Dennis Tobin. The Leeds team was Pat Quinn; George Richardson, Keith McLellan, Lewis Jones, Walter Garside; Gordon Brown, Jeff Stevenson; Tony Skelton, Bernard Prior, Joe Anderson, Colin Tomlinson, Don Robinson and Harry Street.

John Broome had been signed by Widnes in the close season as player coach. He had been part of the famous Wigan team who dominated during the 1950s. John had played in the centre position alongside Ces Mountford at stand off, Tommy Bradshaw at scrum half, with Ernie Ashcroft at centre and wingmen Brian Nordgren and Billy Boston, with Martin Ryan at full back. Not a bad back line!

Frank Myler says, 'John was a major signing for Widnes and he made his intentions clear from the start. He knew Widnes were a good defensive side but, since tries win games, he soon had us practising moving the ball as quickly as possible from the play the ball, as well as the scrum. All the training had changed for the better; we were doing more sprint training and ball practice. The saying, "A change is as good as a rest," prevailed. Widnes improved over the next few seasons, beating many of the leading teams. On a personal note, I would like to thank John for his help and friendship'.

John Smith signed the same year as John Broome. Although only 16 years of age, he was without doubt a future international. Unfortunately, at the age of 18 he had a motor bike accident where he injured his knee and the kneecap was removed. Such an injury in those days usually meant the end of a sportsman's career, but not for John. John's problem was that his knee was permanently rigid and it took over 12 months for him to be able to bend his knee and another 12 months to build up his leg muscles. He eventually signed professional forms for Warrington RLC. Up to the time of his injury, John played scrum half, making his debut at the age of 17. During the period he played for Widnes, John and I played against the best half backs in the game, namely Jeff Stevenson/Lewis Jones, Alex Murphy/Bill Finnan, Albert Cartwright/George Parkinson, Bill Toohey/Willie Horne, Sol Roper/Harry Archer and Rees Thomas/Dave Bolton. John was lucky that Widnes had the best physio in rugby league in Frank Tobin. Frank Tobin served Widnes over 40 years both as fitness coach and physio. During that period he helped to prolong many players' careers by his skill and dedication to both the players and the club. John Smith played for two seasons and then retired. He had shown remarkable pluck and perseverance in the face of adversity and he was a loss to the game.

There were no cup runs in this particular season as Blackpool Borough put Widnes out in the Lancashire Cup first round with a close run 9–4 victory at their Blackpool ground. The Challenge Cup saw the gallant amateurs of Orford Tannery arrive at Naughton Park only to lose 51–2. The tough Workington Town came to Naughton Park in round two and won with the team which took them all the way to Wembley, only to lose out to one of the great Wigan sides in the final. The Workington Town side was Jock McAvoy; Ike Southward, John O'Neill, Danny Leatherbarrow, Bill Wookey; Harry Archer, Sol Roper; Norman Herbert, Bert Eden, Andy Key, Brian Edgar, Ces Thompson and Benny Eve.

Although Widnes did enough to win the game in this difficult cup tie, they were beaten in the end 8–5. The Widnes team that day were Arthur Pimblett; Harry Dawson. John Broome, Bill Thompson, Peter Ratcliffe; Frank Myler, John Smith; Tom Smith, George Kemel, Edgar Bate, Derek Smith, Bob De Witt and Tom Galligan. Bill Thompson scored the Widnes try and Harry Dawson landed the goal.

Frank maintained his form throughout the season and, despite his youth, became a key player for the club. Widnes were renowned as a physical side almost full of local lads who would move heaven and earth to win for the honour of the club and, of course, for the winning pay to supplement their hard earned money from their full time jobs.

This was the season when the Lancashire county selectors noticed this 19 year old bright prospect. The county selectors did this sort of thing in those days. They monitored a promising young player over a season or two and if he attained consistent form, then county selection was near. This process was repeated at international level and, at both county and international level, the abilities of certain players were discussed at meetings. Sometimes 'If you vote for my man, I'll vote for yours' deals were struck between selectors. Other selections were made on the ability of the player, as in Frank's case.

This important season ended with the win at Doncaster in which Frank recorded his hat trick of tries. To consolidate his almost meteoric rise, he required another long season to prove that his physical and mental stamina were up to the rigours of this exhausting nine month timetable. Other players who really did well to play a great amount of games in this season were Harry Dawson, who, along with Frank, played in 40 of the 41 fixtures and Jack Broome, who played in 39. Tom Smith and Edgar Bate, the two props who, playing 37 games and 33 games respectively, did remarkably well for consistency for men playing in those hard days of competitive scrimmaging and hard work loads in the loose. Derek Smith had a grand total of 35 games alternating between open side and blind side second row plus one game at loose forward in a real hard working position. Peter Ratcliffe achieved 37 appearances on the wing which, without having the heavy defensive burden of the stand off or forward positions, was still a great achievement. The loose forward berth was the most populated position as George Kemel, Eddie Myler, Bob Sherman, Tom Galligan, Derek Smith, Vin Smith (Derek Smith's brother), Dennis Tobin, John Thompson and Bill Major pulled on the number 13 jersey during the season.

The great team spirit at the club meant that the players never cried off because that would mean letting their mates down, and it was one of the major reasons for the steady improvement in play during this passing season. In later seasons, when Widnes were given the title 'Cup Kings', their success was cemented by a fierce team spirit and a feeling of family. This spirit was always at the club, and on both good and bad days, Widnes were always a hard team to play and a particularly hard team to beat.

4

A WONDERFUL
1958–59 SEASON

If the previous season had been good for Frank and his excellent playing record then the 1958–59 season was a blockbuster. Missing only three games in the whole season, Frank scored a massive 34 tries. The three games he missed were Keighley at Naughton Park, Rochdale Hornets at the Athletic Grounds and Blackpool Borough, again at home. The team lost the first two games. Keighley won the game at Widnes 14–11 and Hornets won their home game 16–15, Widnes beating Blackpool 40–7. Frank scored four hat tricks and in one game crossed over for four tries. He scored these four tries against Leigh at Naughton Park in their 36–16 win. Each try was a gem in its own right as Frank showed his power, evasive qualities and pace to their best effect. He scored his first hat trick of the season against Salford in the first round of the Lancashire Cup at Widnes, then scored the next two in consecutive weeks against Rochdale Hornets at Widnes and seven days later against Workington Town up in Cumberland.

That fourth hat trick gave Frank great pleasure as it was against one of Widnes's 'bogey' teams, Oldham at Naughton Park. Oldham had developed a habit of beating Widnes in key games, cup ties and the like, but Frank's trio of three pointers came in a resounding 28–6 victory on 11 April and more than made up for the heavy 44–8 defeat at the Watersheddings earlier in the season. Frank's two tries at Whitehaven on 22 November in a magnificent 14–2 win were considered two of the finest seen at the old Recreation Ground in many a year. And so the season went along, with Frank scoring tries, being noticed, yet still only 20 years old.

Not many sides beat Widnes twice that season. The only three teams to do this were Leeds, winning 18–9 at Headingley and 16–5 at Widnes, Keighley winning 14–11 at Widnes and 21–13 at Lawkholme Lane and Warrington winning 17–13 at Naughton Park and 11–7 at Wilderspool. A fine win for Widnes came against Wigan at Central Park in the league when they beat the team 11–7. Wigan were a great side then, deemed particularly strong at home. The game was played on a cold Saturday afternoon in February, and the Wigan side consisted of Fred Griffiths; Billy Boston, Eric Ashton, Keith Holden, Mick Sullivan, Dave Bolton, Rees Thomas; Bill Bretherton, Bill Sayer, Frank Collier, Roy Abram, Brian McTigue and Roy Evans. Widnes, decidedly the underdogs, fielded Arthur Pimblett; Lal Kinsey, John Broome, Bill Thompson, Jimmy Bright; Frank Myler, Brian Keavney; Tom Smith, George Kemel, Edgar Bate, Bob Sherman, Tommy Davies and Bill Major.

Brian Keavney scored the try and Davies kicked three goals and Pimblett one. In the final game of this season, Wigan gained revenge by winning at Naughton Park by a narrow 10–5 margin. Barrow, who had always been a thorn in the Widnes side, were defeated twice by Widnes, 17–8 at Widnes and 9–2 up at Craven Park, Frank scoring the only try of the match. Another fine achievement by Frank was that in the final eight consecutive games of this season he scored at least one try in each game and in total registered 13 tries in those games. People throughout the north, who followed various teams in the Rugby Football League, were all talking about this consistently good scoring stand off, whose defensive qualities matched his attacking prowess.

Like all good players, the opposition paid particular attention to try to stop this phenomenal try-scoring machine. Hit men lined up to take a pot shot at Frank, but the 20 year old could look after himself and although he had to take a few hits, a number of hard men realised their mistake after attempting to take the youngster out. Frank had learned a trick or two in his junior days as a loose forward, and by playing with some handy lads, and soon the hit men left him to play his own brand of football.

A problem of being a match winner at stand off half was that in Frank's time there were some hard hitting stand offs facing a team. These stand offs included the likes of Ray Price of Warrington and St Helens. One had to contend with the fast moving loose forward or open side second rowers. Either could reach a player very quickly indeed. Another dangerous opponent was the opposition inside centre who would stiff arm or hit with his elbow should a player get on the outside of their opposite stand off, just as they were releasing the pass to their outside backs or just as they received a pass! Alan Davies, Oldham and Wigan, was a master of this type of crash tackle, as was Alan Kellett of Oldham and Halifax who would come in from inside centre on the angle to take man and ball.

One can see just how alert and aware young Frank had to be, not only at a scrum where the afore-mentioned attacks could take place but in general broken field play where a forward may be lurking at any time. So whilst the position of stand off half was a glamorous one, it could be very dangerous too. Playing against Frank was difficult as well. He explained in his quiet way that 'I could knock them over in the tackle and look after myself.' Again it is worthwhile remembering Frank's young age at this time and noting that he was a fair way from the full strength he achieved in his mid to late twenties. At this stage, Frank's potential had yet to come to complete fruition. Throughout this period as a shining prospect, he was learning his trade and everything else the game had to throw at him.

To say that the game of rugby league football has many strange twists is an understatement. It is a very simple game which can have the strangest of turns. The old adage from the year dot that suggests that 'when you think you are in, you are out and when you think you are out, you are in', was certainly true for rugby league. Players on many occasions have thought that their consistent good form will bring a representative selection and have been severely disappointed when the call never comes. In Frank's case his consistency at club level, together with his youth, was too obvious for the selectors to miss. As discussed earlier, the selectors spotted a prospect and monitored them for sometimes as long as a couple of seasons. If all the tools were in place after this time, then the player would receive the call for duty. Something else that helped Frank to have a top season was that a regular scrum half played beside him for all but the first seven games.

This was Brian Keavney.

So his terrific season ended with the nagging desire to achieve success in either the County Cup or the Challenge Cup. But there was plenty of time for such a desire to be fulfilled.

5

REPRESENTATIVE
FOOTBALL AT AGE 22

1959–60 season was a real thrill for Frank. Despite not scoring as many tries this term, he developed an edge to his play due to almost two full seasons of uninterrupted first team rugby. The monitoring of his development by the Lancashire county selectors had paid dividends as the Lancashire County Committee desperately wanted ongoing success in the coveted County Championship shield, played for in a triangular tournament between Lancashire, Yorkshire and Cumberland each season. But before any county activity took place, the league programme first had to be adhered to.

The now obligatory game against St Helens was played at Naughton Park with Saints running out 27–14 winners. Four days later Widnes travelled to Central Park to take on Wigan, Frank scoring a try in their very close 16–12 defeat to Wigan. Only three days passed before Widnes were in action again when they went across the hill to play Huddersfield at Fartown. The Fartowners won this one 26–16. On Monday 29 August, Frank scored another try against Barrow, at Naughton Park in the first round of the Lancashire Cup.

Then on 31 August 1959, Frank embarked on his first representative game since playing for Lancashire Schoolboys. About a week before the Barrow cup tie, Frank had received a letter informing him of his selection for the Lancashire County team to play Cumberland at Workington. Not only were Frank and his family delighted, the Widnes club were also thrilled. The Lancashire team set off on the laborious trip up to Workington full of confidence as they were a strong looking side. Frank was also pleased to play alongside his cousin Vince Karalius who was at loose forward. After all, who could provide better protection than Vince was Frank's thought.

The Lancashire team was Austin Rhodes [St Helens]; Bob Greenough [Warrington], Alan Davies [Oldham], Keith Holden [Wigan], Bobby Chisnall [Widnes]; Frank Myler [Widnes], Alex Murphy [St Helens]; John Barton [Wigan], Walt Tabern [Leigh], Ab Terry [St Helens], Brian McTigue [Wigan], Mick Martyn [Leigh] and Vince Karalius [St Helens]. This was a strong Red Rose outfit which, on paper, looked too big and fast for the Cumberland boys to handle. The Cumberland side was Joe Hosking [Leigh]; Aidan Breen [Huddersfield], John O'Neil [Workington Town], Eppie Gibson [Whitehaven], Ron Stephenson [Whitehaven]; Syd Lowden [Salford], Sol Roper [Workington Town]; Bill McAlone [Whitehaven], Alvin Ackerley [Hull Kingston Rovers], Jim Drake [Hull], Bill Drake [Hull], John Tembey [Whitehaven] and Dick Huddart [St Helens].

The set up of the County Championship was that each county played each other. If one of the counties was beaten by the other two then they were out of the running and the two winning counties played off for the Championship. But if all three counties won one each, then points average came into play and the two counties with the better average played off for the Championship. Many considered the County Championship winner's medal to be the most beautiful of all the medals available in the Rugby Football League.

The outcome of Frank's first county game was a 14–8 win for Cumberland. Try scorers for Lancashire were Bob Greenough and Keith Holden with Austin Rhodes kicking a goal. For Cumberland, Aidan Breen and Ron Stephenson scored tries and Syd Lowden landed four goals. The gate was 5,041 and the referee was Mr Eric Clay of Leeds. Frank had a satisfactory debut in the red and white jersey of Lancashire. He had a hand in both of Lancashire's tries and his defence was outstanding.

On 16 September 1959 Cumberland travelled to The Boulevard, Hull, to meet Yorkshire and with a terrific team performance won the County Championship with a 26–13 score line.

So it was back to club football for Frank, two days after the county game, when both he and Bobby Chisnall fronted up with their Widnes team mates against St Helens at Knowsley Road. Saints won easily 22–0 as Widnes went into a five game losing sequence. The Saints game was the first loss, and the team then proceeded to lose 12–10 against Bradford Northern at Odsal, although Frank missed this game. This was followed by a loss at St Helens again in the County Cup at home, Featherstone Rovers gained a good 27–12 win at Naughton Park, then Oldham won at the Watersheddings with a score of 24–12. Frank scored a try in each of the Featherstone and Oldham games. Leigh were beaten by Widnes 24–5 before another big game arose for Frank.

The next game was against the 1959 touring Australians who, because Yorkshire County beat them by a sizable score the previous mid week, played an almost Test strength side against Widnes in the next game. An attendance of over 10,000 saw the game as Widnes were represented by Arthur Pimblett; Bobby Chisnall, Bill Thompson, Derek Heyes, Ray Owen; Frank Myler, Brian Keavney; Tom Smith, Gordon Murray, Edgar Bate, Ken Hill, Arthur Hughes and Bill Major. Again Frank showed up well against this international line up of Australians including Reg Gasnier, Harry Wells, Brian Clay, Barry Muir, Dud Beattie, Ian Walsh, Billy Wilson, Gary Parcell and Brian Hambly. Widnes were overwhelmed at the end of the game as the tourists won 45–15.

It was back to league matches the week after when Widnes beat York at home 28–7. Inconsistent form continued for Widnes as they sustained a heavy 30–13 defeat at Hull Kingston Rovers. This was followed by a 36–0 win at home against Barrow. Another 8–7 defeat at home by Workington was frustrating to the Widnes supporters but they cheered up the following Saturday on seeing their favourites beat Blackpool Borough 20–10. Frank scored four tries in these last three games so he was in form as he approached his 21st birthday in early December. Before his big day there were another few games including his call up for the Lancashire County team to play Yorkshire at Leigh on Wednesday 11 November 1959.

Because Cumberland had beaten Lancashire in August, it was imperative that the Red Rose team won this War of the Roses battle. The game was played at Leigh with a 2.30 p.m. start and the referee was Mr H. Harrison of Horbury. A good crowd of almost 7,000 were in the ground as the teams kicked off and there must have been several thousand sick notes issued in Lancashire that afternoon. The Lancashire team was Eric Fraser [Warrington]; Bobby Greenough, Eric Ashton [Wigan], Alan Davies [Oldham], Jim Challinor [Warrington]; Frank Myler [Widnes], Alex Murphy [St Helens]; John Barton [Wigan], Walt Tabern [Leigh], Brian McTigue [Wigan], Frank Collier [Wigan], Ken Roberts [Swinton] and Laurie Gilfedder [Warrington]. Yorkshire's team was: Frank Dyson [Huddersfield]; Alan Snowden [Halifax], John Burnett [Halifax], Neil Fox [Wakefield Trinity], Cyril Woolford [Featherstone Rovers]; Alan Kellett [Oldham], Jeff Stevenson [York]; Jack Wilkinson [Wakefield Trinity], Milan Kosanovic [Bradford Northern], Don Robinson [Leeds], Brian Briggs [St Helens], Harry Poole [Hunslet] and Fred Ward [Keighley].

The scintillating play by both sides had the crowd roaring. Bobby Greenough sped over for a try and Eric Fraser converted. Then Alan Kellet levelled the score with a fine individual's try and Neil Fox added the extras, then the big centre bulldozed over for a strong try and landed the conversion. Alan Snowden showed his pace with a real wingman's try when he raced away from the Lancashire cover to score under the posts, Fox converting. Frank Myler scored a beautiful try, beating three tacklers in his run, then Frank supported Ken Roberts' break to slice in again under the posts, Eric Fraser landing both goals. The pitch was in perfect condition and this allowed for fast and evasive running from the backs. Frank raced in for his hat trick of tries and Alex Murphy also chipped in with two cracking tries. Eric Fraser landed a total of five goals to give Lancashire 28 points. Yorkshire added tries by Jeff Stevenson (2), Fred Ward, Cyril Woolford and Alan Kellett and Neil Fox banged over seven goals in total to give the White Rose county a 38–28 victory. Lancashire had missed out again in the County Championship.

Frank continued to score tries for Widnes. In 1957–58 he recorded 22 tries, in 1958–59 he scored 34 and in 1959–60 he registered 18. Lack of consistency still bugged Widnes, although from the game against Rochdale Hornets, won at home 14–3 on 14 November, the club had consecutive wins over Barrow away 16–10, Whitehaven home 22–5, Dewsbury home 25–2, a 23–6 defeat at The Willows, Salford, a great

44–11 win over Hull Kingston Rovers, a real hard earned draw at Warrington 9 points all, and a 22–5 win against Liverpool City. The Challenge Cup brought Warrington to Naughton Park in round one and Widnes produced a fine performance to beat The Wire 14–0. This win included a rare drop goal by Frank.

In round two the strong Wakefield Trinity side came to Naughton Park and beat Widnes 5–2 in a very close game. The Wakefield side went on to win the Challenge Cup, beating Hull FC 38–5 at Wembley. The winning Trinity team at Naughton Park was Eric Lockwood; Fred Smith, Alan Skene, Neil Fox, John Etty; Harold Poynton, Keith Holliday; Jack Wilkinson, Geoff Oakes, Malcolm Sampson, Don Vines, Albert Firth and Derek Turner. The Widnes side was Pimblett; Chisnall, Thompson, Kinsey, Heyes; Frank Myler, Keavney; Tom Smith, Kemel, Bate, Winstanley, Chamberlain and Galligan. This game was played in heavy conditions with very little back play. Wakefield's experienced pack laid the foundation for a good win.

Widnes and Frank finished the season in style as they won six of the final seven league games and Frank scored five tries in the last four games. Losing only one of the final seven games, Widnes beat Leigh away, Warrington home, Rochdale Hornets away, Liverpool City away and Salford and Swinton at home. The game they lost was a 15–13 away defeat against York. The season's records showed Widnes played 38 in the league, won 18, drawn 1, lost 19, and again demonstrated the lack of that crucial consistency that they found in later years.

The 1960–61 season was up and down for Widnes. Frank missed a lot of games this season, 13 in all, mainly down to international selection. He had gained another promotion with his selection for the Great Britain World Cup squad for the 1960 World Cup competition. Frank made his Test debut against New Zealand in the first round game at Odsal Stadium, Bradford on 24 September 1960. The Great Britain side in that game was a star studded selection including Eric Fraser [Warrington]; Bobby Greenhough [Warrington], Eric Ashton [Wigan captain], Alan Davies [Oldham], Mick Sullivan [Wigan]; Frank Myler [Widnes], Alex Murphy [St Helens]; Jack Wilkinson [Wakefield Trinity], Tommy Harris [Hull FC], Brian McTigue [Wigan], Vince

Karalius [St Helens], John Whiteley [Hull FC] and Derek Turner [Wakefield Trinity].

The New Zealand team was Cyril Eastlake [Auckland]; Tom Hadfield [Auckland], George Turner [Auckland], Bill Sorenson [Auckland], Neville Denton [Auckland]; George Menzies [West Coast], Keith Roberts [Canterbury]; Henry Maxwell [Auckland], Jock Butterfield [West Coast], Cliff Johnson [Auckland captain], Ron Ackland [Auckland], Trevor Kilkelly [West Coast] and Mel Cooke [Canterbury]. The referee was Monsieur Edouard Martung of Bordeaux.

Great Britain took the unusual step of playing three loose forwards in this game, Vince Karalius and John Whiteley in the second row and Derek Turner in the number 13 jersey. Despite winning their share of ball from the set scrum, the envisaged sweeping passing movements in midfield did not happen. The invention of playing three loose forwards did not go to plan. The British forwards kept the ball tight with their fast and elusive backs seeing little of the ball in the first half. Eric Fraser landed four goals in this game with tries from Alex Murphy, from a great break by Vince Karalius supported by John Whiteley and finished in style by the quicksilver Murphy. A Frank Myler special came from a Murphy and Eric Ashton move which culminated in Frank beating two Kiwi tacklers in his run to the line. Then a three man move begun by Brian McTigue's strong burst in midfield and ending with a neat little 'scissors' move between Frank and Vince Karalius saw Frank deliver a perfect long pass for Eric Ashton to stride in from 30 yards. These were just three of the five tries scored by the British as Vince Karalius and Eric Ashton worked brilliantly together to serve Alan Davies who was almost unstoppable in his dash for a fourth try. Brian McTigue tidied things up with a dummying run of 25 yards to register the fifth try. Mel Cooke scored the Kiwi's try with Bill Sorenson kicking a goal. This was Great Britain's first ever World Cup win on home soil and how the Odsal crowd of 20,600 enjoyed it!

Seven days later, Great Britain played France in the second round of the World Cup at the magnificent Station Road, Swinton. Cock-a-hoop over their success against the Kiwis, Great Britain introduced four changes to the side, giving runs to other members of their squad.

The team was Eric Fraser [Warrington]; Jim Challinor [Warrington], Austin Rhodes [St Helens], Alan Davies [Oldham], Mick Sullivan [Wigan]; Frank Myler [Widnes], Alex Murphy [St Helens]; Jack Wilkinson [Wakefield Trinity], John 'Jobey' Shaw [Halifax], Brian McTigue [Wigan], Brian Shaw [Hunslet], Vince Karalius [St Helens] and John Whiteley [Hull FC captain]. France featured Louis Poletti [Carcassonne]; Jacques Dubon [Villeneuve], Roger Rey [Avignon], Claude Mantoulan [Roanne], Raymond Gruppi [Villeneuve]; Jacques Merquey [Villeneuve], Joseph Guiraud [Montpellier]; Aldo Quaglio [Roanne], Andre Casas [Perpignan], Robert Eramouspe [Roanne], Jean Barthe [Roanne captain], Yeve Mezard [Cavaillon] and Andre Lacaze [Toulouse]. The referee was once again Monsieur Edouard Martung of Bordeaux.

The British forwards laid a great foundation for this 33–7 win in which the team scored seven excellent tries and Eric Fraser landed six goals. Vince Karalius, John Whiteley and Brian McTigue opened up the French defence for Alan Davies to cross after 10 minutes' play, then a terrific break by skipper Whiteley supported by Brian McTigue allowed the ball handling prop to send his front row partner, Jack Wilkinson, tearing over. Mick Sullivan registered the third try after magical play between Brian McTigue and Vince Karalius, a typical Frank Myler effort added the fourth try after Frank's tackle forced Jacques Merquey to spill the ball and the Widnes man then kicked the loose ball ahead to win the race for the touchdown by the corner flag.

Tremendous work between forwards and backs allowed Alan Davies to score his second, and Britain's fifth, try and Austin Rhodes showed his classy St Helens form by crossing for the final two tries of the game. Jacques Dubon scored France's only try with Andre Lacaze kicking two goals. As Great Britain pulled away into a winning lead, the French, understandably, became frustrated and one or two niggling incidents occurred. The biggest was a stand up fight between the French captain Jean Barthe and Vince Karalius. There could only be one winner there of course and Barthe was laid prostrate whilst the remainder of the British pack stood shoulder to shoulder taking on the French forwards. When one studies the British pack that day, one must admire the courage of the French forwards because six tough men represented Great Britain on the Station Road pitch that afternoon. Vince and Jean were sent off for their gladiatorial battle. It says it all when Vince walked off the pitch whilst Jean was assisted off.

The deciding game in this rough, yet totally enjoyable, World Cup was held on 8 October 1960. Both Great Britain and Australia had beaten France and New Zealand in the previous rounds so this encounter was literally the World Cup final. Frank was in a particularly rich vein of form and his partnership at half back with the mercurial Alex Murphy produced one of the outstanding half back pairings of recent times. So much was at stake in this match. The ground conditions at Odsal, on this day of almost continuous tropical rain, were dreadful! According to Robert Gate's superb history, *Rugby League Lions, 100 years of Test Matches*, the playing area was 'a squelchy and treacherous pitch, and Australia fell into the trap of taking Britain on up front instead of using their match winning backs'.

The Great Britain team on duty that day was Austin Rhodes [St Helens]; Billy Boston [Wigan], Eric Ashton [Wigan captain], Alan Davies [Oldham], Mick Sullivan [Wigan]; Frank Myler [Widnes], Alex Murphy [St Helens]; Jack Wilkinson [Wakefield Trinity], John 'Jobey' Shaw [Halifax], Brian McTigue [Wigan], Brian Shaw [Hunslet], Derek Turner [Wakefield Trinity] and Vince Karalius [St Helens]. The Aussies selected from strength and played Keith Barnes [Balmain captain]; Ron Boden [Parramatta], Reg Gasnier [St George], Harry Wells [Western Suburbs], Brian Carlson [North Sydney]; Tony Brown [Newtown], Barry Muir [Brisbane Wests]; Dud Beattie [Ipswich], Noel Kelly [Ipswich], Gary Parcell [Ipswich], Rex Mossop [Manly], Elton Rasmussen [Toowoomba] and Brian Hambly [Wagga-Wagga].

The referee was once again the highly respected Monsieur Edouard Martung of Bordeaux and the attendance was 33,000. Robert Gate also recalls the sentiments of top rugby league writers of the day, Tom Longworth and Derek Marshall, whose considered opinions were accepted back in 1960. Longworth declared, 'This was rugby league in its ugliest form' and Marshall called it 'an example of skulduggery in which players were kicked, hacked and hit in a manner which must have repelled those watching on TV. The game produced a sustained brand of viciousness I hope never to see again'. This was, after all, a full bloodied World Cup Final between the two top nations, in the hardest team game of all, for the top prize of all. It was almost the equivalent of winning a Test series and that would be enough for any supporter of the game to accept the hardness of the occasion! This World Cup decider went the way of Great Britain due mainly to the magnificent determination of the British side, led by a great forward display, two strong, quick half backs and a general, backs-to-the-wall team effort.

Britain's two tries were claimed by their wingmen, Billy Boston racing over for the first after Vince Karalius found Eric Ashton with a fine wide pass and the centre had Billy 'B' crashing past the Aussie cover for a cracking try in the corner. Austin Rhodes converted this try with a monster of a goal from the morass. Vince Karalius again had a hand in the try by Mick Sullivan when he had Alex Murphy zooming onto one of Vince's special passes. The electric quick scrum half fed 'Sulli' at just the right time for the wingman to race 40 yards to score a fine try, despite having been laid out in a tackle only 15 minutes earlier, and suffering from a slight concussion. The Aussie stand off half Tony Brown created a fine try for Brian Carlson on the hour, but Keith Barnes found the distance for the conversion too great.

So the Great Britain side won the World Cup and snatched the trophy and the title of World Champions from the grasp of the Australians. This seemed to be the start of Frank's success for Great Britain and it is strange to think that ten years later in the World Cup of 1970 that Frank Myler would be captain of the British World Cup squad.

There were some good results in the league programme for Widnes as well as some not so good ones. Frank had seven games with Widnes before he was called up again for the international game against France at Stade Municipal in Bordeaux on 11 December 1960. France were smarting over their 33–7 World Cup defeat at Swinton and selected a strong side in an attempt to regain some pride against the current World Cup winners. Great Britain went for a tried and tested squad although they did recall St Helens front rower Abe Terry and gave a first cap to John Barton, Wigan's big prop. The side was Eric Fraser

[Warrington captain]; Billy Boston [Wigan], Neil Fox [Wakefield Trinity], Alan Davies [Oldham], Mick Sullivan [Wigan]; Frank Myler [Widnes], Alex Murphy [St Helens]; Abe Terry [St Helens], 'Jobey' Shaw [Halifax], John Barton [Wigan], Brian Shaw [Hunslet], Derek Turner [Wakefield Trinity] and Vince Karalius [St Helens]. France held their faith in the 'old brigade' and selected Louis Poletti [Carcassonne]; Raymond Gruppi [Villeneuve], Jean Foussat [Villeneuve], Roger Rey [Avignon], Andre Savonne [Avignon]; Claude Mantoulan [Roanne], Georges Fages [Albi]; Jean Pano [Villeneuve], Antranick Apelian [Marseille], Aldo Quaglio [Roanne], Jean Barthe [Roanne captain], Robert Eramouspe [Roanne] and Andre Lacaze [Toulouse].

Great Britain played like World Cup winners! Running the ball in devastating fashion and tackling like demons proved winning factors for Great Britain, despite a huge deficit in ball from the scrum. This was because Georges Fages was allowed to feed the scrums as is the fashion today, in behind the legs of his second row forwards! The referee, Monsieur Georges Jameau blandly called 'Play on!' to each complaint offered by the British front row. Despite being swamped in the scrum, 'Jobey' Shaw had a blinder in the loose. Andre Lacaze gave France the lead with an early penalty, then centre Jean Foussat released his wingman, Raymond Gruppi to go in powerfully for a good unconverted try. Billy Boston picked up a loose ball and blasted his way through on a 30 yard run. Boston found Frank Myler in support and Frank continued the move with Derek Turner. As the cover converged on Turner, the loose forward ran across Frank and delivered the perfect back pass which allowed Frank to run in between the posts for a fine try which Eric Fraser converted. Just on half time Lacaze added a penalty goal to send France in with a lead of 7–5.

Neil Fox used his awesome power to break a tackle and score an excellent try after great approach work by Alex Murphy and Vince Karalius. Billy Boston went on another rampaging run to link with 'Jobey' Shaw who, in turn, fed Alex Murphy. 'Murph' drew Poletti and served Neil Fox who crossed near the corner flag. Murphy, in irrepressible form, flashed over for the fourth try and Frank Myler ran superbly to make the final try for 'Jobey' Shaw, and Neil Fox rounded off the British scoring with two goals. For France, Jean Foussat crashed over in the final moments, and was awarded a try that the Brits disputed as they were adamant that he had dropped the ball over the try line.

Widnes had the misfortune to play St Helens five times in this term, twice in the league, once in the Lancashire Cup and twice in the Challenge Cup. The reason they played Widnes twice in the Challenge Cup was that Widnes fought out a tremendously brave draw, 5 points all, at Knowsley Road in the first round only to lose the replay at Naughton Park 29–10. The Lancashire Cup tie was played at Widnes and again the black and whites were unlucky not to win as they went down 19–17. In the league Saints really turned up the heat in their home league game winning 44–7, this game was played immediately after the two Challenge Cup ties. The Saints team that day was Austin Rhodes (7 goals); Tom van Vollenhoven (5 tries), Ken Large (1 try), Brian McGinn, Mick Sullivan (1 try); Wilf Smith, Alex Murphy (1 try); Abe Terry, Bob Dagnall, Jim Measures, Don Vines, Dick Huddart (2 tries) and Vince Karalius. The final game between the clubs was much closer, Saints winning 17–5. Widnes did the double over Huddersfield and fought through a titanic game in the mud in November to beat Wigan 5–3 at Naughton Park.

Representative football called out again to Frank when he was selected to play for Lancashire against Yorkshire at Wakefield on 31 August 1960. There was a determination about this Lancashire side who seemed very confident against a strong White Rose team who, of course, were playing on home soil. The Yorkshire selectors were always willing to play local players in inter-county games as it built up the gate. In this game, four Wakefield Trinity players and one former star Trinity man were selected. The Yorkshire side was Frank Dyson [Huddersfield]; Fred Smith [Wakefield Trinity], John Burnett [Halifax], Neil Fox [Wakefield Trinity], Mick Sullivan [Wigan]; Alan Kellett [Oldham], Jeff Stevenson [York]; Jack Wilkinson [Wakefield Trinity], John 'Jobey' Shaw [Halifax], Don Robinson [Leeds], Terry Clawson [Featherstone Rovers], John Whiteley [Hull FC] and Derek Turner [Wakefield Trinity]. Don Robinson, then at Leeds, was the former Trinity man so the home club was well represented. Lancashire also had a strong side in Eric Fraser [Warrington]; Bobby Greenough [Warrington], Alan Davies [Oldham], Jim Challinor [Warrington], Trevor Simms [Rochdale Hornets]; Frank Myler [Widnes], Alex Murphy [St Helens]; John Barton [Wigan], Walt Tabern [Leigh], Brian McTigue [Wigan], Frank Collier [Wigan], Laurie Gilfedder [Warrington] and Bill Major [Widnes]. The referee was Mr Charlie Appleton of Warrington, and the gate was a healthy 15,045.

This was one of the better inter-county games, with cameo performances from all the key players. The battle at half back between Frank and Alex Murphy and Alan Kellett and Jeff Stevenson was worth the entrance fee. In the forwards, Frank Collier and John Whiteley were outstanding and the ball playing of Brian McTigue created problems for Yorkshire. Lancashire took the honours in a real nail biter with a 21–20 win. Frank Collier (2), Alan Davies (2) and Bobby Greenough scored Lancashire's tries with Eric Fraser (2) and Laurie Gilfedder kicking goals. For Yorkshire John Burnett, Alan Kellett and John Whiteley (2) scored tries and Neil Fox landed four goals.

This fine win by Lancashire meant that if they were to beat Cumberland then they would be County Champions. It was considered quite an achievement in those days to win this inter-county trophy as it gave good natured bragging rights to the winning county committees. The keepsake for the winning players was the ornate gold medal which was highly valued amongst players of the time. The 1960–61 County Championship was unusual because the competition was extended in time to allow for the 1960 World Cup. The Lancashire v Yorkshire tie was played in August 1960 and the second tie, Lancashire v Cumberland, was played at Salford on 27 May 1961!

This meant there was one match at the start of the season and one at the end. Lancashire played Cumberland and, as stated, had to beat them to win the Championship. The Lancashire team at The Willows, or Weaste as it was known then, was Eric Fraser [Warrington]; Bobby Greenough [Warrington], Alan Davies [Oldham], Eric Ashton [Wigan], Trevor Simms [Rochdale Hornets]; Frank Myler [Widnes], Alex Murphy [St Helens]; John Barton [Wigan], Trevor Roberts [Swinton], Brian McTigue [Wigan], Frank Collier [Wigan], Laurie Gilfedder [Warrington] and Bill Major [Widnes]. Cumberland selected the following side, Syd Lowden [Workington Town]; Ike Southward [Workington Town], John O'Neil [Workington Town], Eddie Brennan [Workington Town], Aidan Breen [Huddersfield]; Phil Kitchen [Whitehaven], Sol Roper [Workington Town]; Ray Donaldson [Whitehaven], Malcolm Moss [Workington Town], Bill Martin [Workington Town], Bill Drake [Hull FC], Dick Huddart [Saints] and Don Wilson [Barrow]. Attendance was 6,000 and the man with the whistle was Mr Eric Clay of Leeds.

Lancashire attacked with a superb display of fast open football that had the Cumberland boys back peddling. The classy play of Eric Ashton made a magnificent hat trick of tries for the speedy Trevor Simms. Frank Myler and Alex Murphy both raced in for tries and the Lancastrian pack contributed with tries by Trevor Roberts, Brian McTigue and Laurie Gilfedder. Eric Fraser chipped in with four goals to give Lancashire 32 points against Cumberland's 18. Phil Kitchen, Syd Lowden, John O'Neil and Eddie Brennan scored tries and Brennan (2) and Ike Southward kicked their goals. The County Championship and those gorgeous medals went to the Red Rose players of Lancashire.

A county selection was a great achievement with so many good players around back then. The Lancashire side in this Championship winning season had some of the most outstanding players in the whole country and some who rated as possibly the best ever in their positions. Alex Murphy, Frank Myler, Brian McTigue, Eric Ashton, Alan Davies and Frank Collier were household names in all three rugby league playing counties. Cumberland also had international players in Phil Kitchen, Ike Southward, Bill Martin, Bill Drake and the kingpin back rower Dick Huddart. They had other players who would have had a regular international career in any other age, Sol Roper, Syd Lowden, Don Wilson and Aidan Breen to mention just a few.

The 1960 World Cup disrupted the County Championship but in 1961 the touring Kiwis arrived. This was three months after the great Lancashire championship winning game. It was back to club football for Frank as Widnes finished off this 1960–61 term. There were some big wins for Widnes towards the end of the season as well as one or two bad results. Clear wins over York at home, 30–15, Barrow at home

26–13, Liverpool City at home 23–0, Salford at home 30–9 and one result that was pleasing was the win over Hunslet at Naughton Park after a 32–0 drubbing at Parkside in September, a game in which Frank did not play.

Frank did play in the return game at Widnes and the Chemics cleaned the slate with an exciting 22–10 win. This game had some of the best football played in all the season and in this thrilling win the Widnes side was Arthur Pimblett; Bobby Chisnall, Jimmy Bright, Bill Thompson, Harry Dawson; Frank Myler, Brian Keavney; Tom Smith, Geoff Smart, Edgar Bate, Ronnie Bate, Brian Winstanley and Tommy Galligan. Try scorers for Widnes were Frank, Bobby Chisnall, Bill Thompson and Arthur Pimblett with Harry Dawson landing five goals. The Hunslet team was Billy Langton; Colin Byrom, Geoff Shelton, Jim Stockdill, Willie Walker; Alan Preece, Dennis Tate; Wilf Adams, Sam Smith, Don Hatfield, Keith Whitehead, Geoff Gunney and Ian Robinson. For Hunslet, Geoff Shelton crossed twice for tries and Billy Langton kicked two goals. The final game of the season ended in a 10–4 win for Widnes over Huddersfield at Fartown.

6

LEADING THE WAY
TO FURTHER
INTERNATIONALS

In 1961 Frank had other things on his mind as well as football. In June that year he married his long time girlfriend, Eileen Lucas. He and Eileen had been courting since they were about 16, so Eileen was well used to the demands that rugby made on Frank's time. They were married on a Thursday, which meant that many of the guests had to take a day off work to attend the wedding. However, that didn't deter anyone from attending and, on the big day, St Marie's RC Church in Widnes was filled with family and friends. To add an extra special touch to the occasion the ceremony was conducted by Frank's mother's cousin, Fr Vincent Karalius, who travelled to Widnes from Leigh where he was a parish priest.

The first game of the 1961–62 season was fairly momentous, as it was against the touring New Zealanders. Some teams joined forces to play the tourists, as this tour was a short one of only 20 games. Teams who combined to play the New Zealanders were Castleford-Featherstone Rovers, a Leeds XIII, Oldham-Rochdale Hornets, a Manchester XIII, Huddersfield-Halifax, Hull FC-Hull Kingston Rovers and Whitehaven-Workington Town. The two teams missing from that list were Widnes-Liverpool City. Liverpool supplied three players, Ray Ashby, Bob Burdell and George Walker, and Widnes the remainder, Bob Randall, Bobby Chisnall, Bill Thompson, Jim Bright, Frank Myler, Wally Hurstfield, Edgar Bate, Brian Winstanley, Tommy

Galligan and Arthur Hughes.

Having so many Widnes players in the mix was a help to the team especially when Frank Myler scored the home try. He used his pace off the mark, then his strength and experience to cross the Kiwi line in style. Fellow Widnes team mate Randall landed three goals in the 9–6 win. Frank was out injured for five games after the match against the Kiwis but returned in the centre position for Batley's visit to score a try in the 27–0 victory. Frank was still in the centre when Widnes beat Wigan in the second round of the Lancashire Cup 9–5 at Naughton Park but was back at stand off for the big win over Bradford Northern at Odsal, where Frank crossed the Northern try line twice in the 33–2 victory. On 13 September, Frank played for Lancashire County against the Kiwis at Warrington. A crowd of 10,000 watched a game controlled by referee Mr Harry Pickersgill of Castleford.

The Kiwis didn't have a particularly good tour results wise. Overall their tour record read played 20, won 8, lost 12. When they came to Wilderspool in Warrington to play Lancashire in the eighth game of the tour, they had lost four and won three. More to the point, they were only three games away from the first Test and the Rugby Football League were worried that the supporters of the game might not want to come to see a whitewash in a Test match. It was hoped that the Kiwis would find some form against a strong Lancashire team, to give some confidence to the supporters to attend the first Test match. The Lancashire County side was Eric Fraser [Warrington]; Bill Burgess [Barrow], Eric Ashton [Wigan], Bobby Greenough [Warrington], Trevor Simms [Rochdale Hornets]; Frank Myler [Widnes], Alex Murphy [Saints]; John Barton [Wigan], Trevor Roberts [Swinton], Brian McTigue [Wigan], Peter Norburn [Swinton], Laurie Gilfedder [Warrington] and Dave Parker [Oldham]. New Zealand put out a strong looking side with a big pack with Sam Edwards and 'Maunga' Emery the two huge Maori props. The team was, Jack Fagan; Brian Reidy, Reg Cooke, Roger Bailey, Allen Amer; Jim Bond, Bill Snowden; Sam Edwards, Jock Butterfield, Maunga Emery, Mel Cooke, Bruce Castle and Brian Lee.

The game was interrupted by several fights and one big brawl. Mr Pickersgill handled the brawl well and after that, fighting was only spasmodic. In between the punching and butting, Lancashire played some good football but the Kiwis were still finding that their good form was at a premium. Both sides scored three tries, Eric Ashton, John Barton and Alex Murphy for Lancashire and Brian Reidy, Roger Bailey and Brian Lee for the Kiwis. It was the goal kicking that won it for Lancashire with Eric Fraser kicking one goal and Laurie Gilfedder kicking two with Jack Fagan landing two goals giving Lancashire the spoils by 15–13. In general play, Frank and Alex Murphy had the legs on the Kiwi half backs, Jim Bond and Bill Snowden. Dave Parker, in at loose forward, also had a fine game. The New Zealanders took great heart from this result, and went on to beat a combined Huddersfield-Halifax side by 31–11, and almost unbelievably beat Great Britain in the first Test 29–11 at Headingley! Our national side did recover and win the next two Tests to take the series 2 games to 1. But the central counties of Yorkshire and Lancashire beat the tourists fair and square with Yorkshire also beating the Kiwis 21–11. Once again it was back to his club for Frank, and back into the hard grind of league football.

Widnes did the double over Barrow this season and actually beat Whitehaven three times, home and away in the league and in the first round of the County Cup. Frank crossed the line for 11 tries for Widnes this term and on 17 March, the Widnes board brought a great player to the club when they completed the transfer of Vince Karalius from St Helens. Frank and Vince were first cousins and with Vince stiffening up the pack, things looked good for Widnes.

The week of 7–14 October was a busy one for Frank. On 7 October came a defeat at home to Huddersfield 18–8 and on 14 October came another 16–2 defeat this time against Swinton at Station Road. In between these two games on the Wednesday, was another county game against Yorkshire at Hilton Park, Leigh. The referee for this game was the former Wakefield Trinity, Featherstone Rovers and Hunslet forward Laurie Gant of Wakefield. He went on later to be a successful coach taking Featherstone Rovers to a winning Wembley final against Barrow. Laurie was a cobbler in the village of Wrenthorpe near Wakefield, and was Neil Fox's personal boot repairer. He used to build up the left boot toe cap into a square of leather for the great goal kicker.

The county game was a straight play off for second place, as both Yorkshire and Lancashire had been beaten by Cumberland. Both counties fancied their chances and selected strong teams. Yorkshire relied on Cyril Kellett [Hull Kingston Rovers]; Gary Waterworth [Featherstone Rovers], Derek Hallas [Leeds], Neil Fox [Wakefield Trinity], Mick Sullivan [St Helens]; Brian Gabbitas [Hunslet], Keith Holliday [Wakefield Trinity]; Les Hammill [Featherstone Rovers], Allan Lockwood [Dewsbury], Ken Noble [Huddersfield], Jack Fairbank [Leeds], Geoff Gunney [Hunslet] and John Whiteley [Hull FC]. Lancashire selected a merciless pack and had pace on the wings, strength and pace in the centres and half backs who had been team mates in the successful 1958 tour of Australia. The team was Ken Gowers [Swinton]; Trevor Simms [Rochdale Hornets], Johnny Noon [Oldham], Frank Myler [Widnes], Terry O'Grady [Warrington]; Dave Bolton [Wigan], Alex Murphy [St Helens]; Bill Payne [Oldham], Trevor Roberts [Swinton], Frank Collier [Wigan], Mick Martyn [Leigh], Laurie Gilfedder [Warrington] and Arthur Hughes [Widnes].

The mostly Lancastrian attendance was 5,000 and they cheered every move and tackle made by their heroes. The strong suit of the Lancashire side was their pace in the middle of the field and that was where the damage was done to the slightly slower Yorkshire backs. Johnny Noon accepted the pass on the end of a cross field passing movement to register a try. Frank sliced through from a scrum to score a beauty and Dave Bolton was too quick on his feet for Brian Gabbitas as he stepped his way over. Alex Murphy produced one of his specials in a 40 yards dash to score and Laurie Gilfedder landed one goal to give Lancashire their 14 points. Yorkshire replied by sending Gary Waterworth over in the corner and Neil Fox, a powerful player, took a couple of tacklers over with him when scoring his try. Neil Fox also added three goals but the verdict went to Lancashire with a grand 14–12 win. Lancashire's pack played a big part in the win as Roberts edged Lockwood in the scrums to give the smart footballers, Myler, Bolton and Murphy, the time and position to work their skills to the best of their ability. The teams played the afternoon game in typical October weather with a strong, cold wind blowing throughout.

On 10 February, Widnes were knocked out of the Challenge Cup by Leigh at Hilton Park and in the following 16 games to the season's end they won 12 and lost only four. Included in these wins was a victory over Wigan at Naughton Park by 12–10. Frank played in 29 of the 40 Widnes games that season, five in the centre and the remainder at stand off half. When not at number six, Ged Lowe played there. Ged was a fine utility player who served Widnes well both at stand off and in the centre. The Widnes backs of that era were all adaptable three quarters with the centres coming from several players who were classed as regular first team players. Bill Thompson, Jim Bright, Derek Heyes, Lal Kinsey, Ged Lowe and Frank all turned out in the centres, Bobby Chisnall, Johnny Gaydon, Harry Dawson, Jim Bright and Ged Lowe featured in the wing positions whilst the regular full back was Bob Randall who missed only one game that season. The scrum halves were Brian Keavney, Ray Owen and Derek Heyes.

In March 1962, the international selectors met to choose the touring squad for the trip to Australia and New Zealand in the coming summer. Frank's current form and his ability to be able to play in several positions in the backs made him a firm favourite for a seat on the plane. He had also become a 'regular' in the Lancashire County side which was considered then as a natural stepping stone to international recognition.

The normal course of selection for a tour was to take two players for each position, giving a squad of 26 men. It was also the norm to take at least a couple of 'utility' players, ones who could play at a high level in more than one set position. Frank seemed certain to gain selection on this ability alone. His two biggest challengers for the number six jersey were Dave Bolton [Wigan] and Harold Poynton [Wakefield Trinity] but Frank currently held that crucial stand off role for Lancashire County, which appeared to be a huge plus. All touring sides selected used to throw up at least one player who was a complete surprise to the supporters of the game who eagerly awaited the publication of the touring squad. When the side was announced, the shock was not who had gained selection but who had been omitted. Three players expected to gain certain selection, Frank, Alan Davies [Oldham] and Ken Gowers [Swinton] would not be travelling.

Despite having a placid and sensible nature, Frank was upset at being overlooked. In his own mind he had done enough to have gained selection. As Frank expected, Bolton and Poynton received the call. The shock selections to make the tour were full back-centre Gary Cooper [Featherstone Rovers], centre Peter Small [Castleford] and prop forward Ken Noble [Huddersfield]. Frank, at 23 years of age, should have made that selection as his play in the Test trial and the inter-county games had been perfect and his club form outstanding. Luckily Frank's phlegmatic nature accepted this situation and, although disappointed, he took the attitude that there was another tour in 1966 and he was easily young enough to make that. Widnes took advantage of being invited to play two exhibition games in Dublin in May 1962 against Featherstone Rovers and Huddersfield and Frank enjoyed the relaxing closed season break.

The 1962–63 season was a big one for Frank. It was also a unique one for the Rugby Football League as the league reverted to two divisions. To make up for the loss in revenue, the league introduced a Western and an Eastern Competition played at the start of the season. Widnes were in one of the Western leagues which included Rochdale Hornets, Liverpool City, Whitehaven and Barrow. In this new concept, Widnes beat all the teams, home and away, except Barrow up at Craven Park.

Widnes gained revenge when Barrow came down to Naughton Park and Widnes won 39–7. The good results in this new competition took Widnes into the semi final of the Western Competition to play the mighty St Helens at Knowsley Road. The St Helens team on that day was Kel Coslett; Tom van Vollenhoven, Keith Northy, Mick Sullivan, Len Killeen; Billy Benyon, Wilf Smith; John Arkwright, Bob Dagnall, Cliff Watson, John Temby, Dick Huddart and Harry Major. Widnes selected from strength and had the great Vince Karalius playing on the ground where he made his name. The team was Bob Randall; Bobby Chisnall, Jim Bright, Bill Thompson, Derek Heyes; Frank Myler, Ray Owen; Wally Hurstfield, George Kemel, Edgar Bate, Ronnie Bate, Jim Measures and Vince Karalius. Frank scored a sensational try as did Jim Measures, Randall landing two goals. Cliff Watson scored a try for Saints and Kel Coslett kicked one goal and landed two drop goals. Vince Karalius put in a performance that had the 20,000 spectators gasping: he was everywhere on the field.

Widnes went to the Western Competition final on the back of a brilliant 10–9 win. After the victory over Rochdale Hornets on the opening day of the season, Frank was notified of his selection, yet again, for the Lancashire County side to play Cumberland at Widnes in the County Championship. This was on 12 September 1962. The season started on 18 August and meant that Frank played in six games in 20 days as he missed the opening game against Rochdale.

The game before the county match was the first round of the Lancashire Cup against Swinton at Station Road. In an iron hard cup tie, Swinton ended up the victors by the narrow margin of 5–2, the score reflecting just how challenging this game had been. The Lancashire team was one of the most interesting selections made for some time and comprised of Ken Gowers [Swinton]; Bill Burgess [Barrow], Alan Davies [Wigan], Alan Buckley [Swinton], Trevor Simms [Oldham]; Frank Myler [Widnes], Jacky Edwards [Warrington]; John Barton [Wigan], Bill Sayer [Wigan], Frank Collier [Wigan], Jim Measures [Widnes], Ray French [St Helens] and Vince Karalius [Widnes]. The combination of Frank Myler, Jacky Edwards and Vince Karalius behind a pack that were going forward was the key to success. The Cumberland side was Syd Lowden [Workington Town]; Joe Mossop [Whitehaven], Eddie Brennan [Workington Town], John O'Neil [Workington Town], Tom McNally [Workington Town]; Harry Archer [Workington Town], Sol Roper [Workington Town]; Jim Drake [Hull Kingston Rovers], Tom Hill [Whitehaven], Bill Martin [Workington Town], Matt McLeod [Workington Town], John Temby [St Helens] and Bill Drake [Hull FC]. The referee was Mr Matt Coates of Pudsey and the attendance at Naughton Park was 8,000.

Lancashire proved too strong for Cumberland and ran out 28–8 winners. Bill Burgess scored four tries and Frank and Trevor Simms one apiece with Ken Gowers landing five goals. For Cumberland, Eddie Brennan and big Matt McLeod crossed for tries and Syd Lowden kicked a goal. Frank had another fine game against the tenacious tackling Harry Archer.

Leeds were beaten 15–2 at Headingley, then after the great win at Saints, Warrington were beaten at Widnes 20–5 as 'The Chemics' continued their excellent start to the season. Wakefield Trinity fell 13–

10 at Belle Vue, then Widnes claimed a terrific double when they beat Leeds 13–12 at Widnes. The second County Championship game came around quickly and was played at Belle Vue, Wakefield. It took place on 26 September and to claim the Championship, Lancashire had to beat this strong Yorkshire side. The White Rose committee were also determined to win the Championship. The Yorkshire side was: Frank Dyson [Huddersfield]; Geoff Smith [York], Geoff Shelton [Hunslet], Neil Fox [Wakefield Trinity], Duncan Jackson [Halifax]; Dave Elliott [Hull Kingston Rovers], Carl Dooler [Featherstone Rovers]; Les Hammill [Featherstone Rovers], Don Close [Huddersfield], Brian Tyson [Hull Kingston Rovers], Brian Briggs [Wakefield Trinity], Terry Clawson [Featherstone Rovers] and Fred Ward [Hunslet]. Lancashire went mainly with the side that beat Cumberland so convincingly but had Ian Hodgkiss of Leigh on the wing for Bill Burgess and Brian McTigue in a rearranged pack with Ray French dropping out. The Lancashire side was: Ken Gowers [Swinton]; Ian Hodgkiss [Leigh], Alan Davies [Wigan], Alan Buckley [Swinton], Trevor Simms [Oldham]; Frank Myler [Widnes], Jacky Edwards [Warrington]; John Barton [Wigan], Bill Sayer [Wigan], Brian McTigue [Wigan], Frank Collier [Wigan], Jim Measures [Widnes] and Vince Karalius [Widnes]. The referee was the excellent Mr D.T.H Davies of Manchester and the attendance was 7,956.

Whilst Yorkshire won the game by a convincing score, in fact the White Rose outfit scored four tries against two from Lancashire. The large difference in the score line were the five goals kicked by that master goal kicker, Neil Fox. The result for the record was Yorkshire 22, Lancashire 8. Ian Hodgkiss raced over for a debut try and big Frank Collier used his power to register another try to go with Ken Gowers' one goal giving Lancashire their eight points. Frank Dyson, Geoff Smith (2) and Geoff Shelton scored the four tries for Yorkshire who, having already beaten Cumberland, claimed the County Championship.

Back at Widnes, Frank and the team prepared for the first ever Western Competition final. Their opponents were the sturdy Workington Town, and the game was at Central Park, Wigan on 10 November 1962. The Widnes team was Bob Randall; Bobby Chisnall, Ged Lowe, Bill Thompson, Derek Heyes; Frank Myler, Ray Owen;

Wally Hurstfield, George Kemel, Edgar Bate, Ronnie Bate, Jim Measures and Vince Karalius. Frank had an extra shot of confidence as he found out in the week before the Workington game that he had been selected for the full England team to play France at Headingley on 17 November, one week after the Western Championship decider.

In a real ruthless final, the score at full time was Widnes 9 Workington Town 9. A replay would be held, again at Central Park, on Wednesday 21 November four days after Frank's debut for England. The first final was a hum-dinger of a game with brutal defence on both sides. Thompson scored the Widnes try with Bob Randall kicking three goals. Workington were well represented by all their Cumberland county players who, fortunately, were fit and able. The players included Syd Lowden, Eddie Brennan, John O'Neil, Harry Archer, Sol Roper, Bill Martin and Matt McLeod and the two international forwards, Norman Herbert and Brian Edgar. Both sides could have won the game.

On the day of the international game, Widnes played Warrington at Wilderspool and lost 15–4, Ged Lowe filling in for Frank. Across the country at Headingley, Frank was pulling on the white jersey of England for the first time. It appeared that he had served his apprenticeship and the door might open for further representative selections and possibly even a call up for Great Britain! But first things first, he had to play well for England. The England side selected was a rugged, no nonsense, solid one with bags of experience in the correct places. On Frank's outside were the two best men at the time, Eric Ashton and Neil Fox and on his inside, the worldly wise Tommy Smales. The side was Ken Gowers [Swinton]; Bill Burgess [Barrow], Eric Ashton [Wigan], Neil Fox [Wakefield Trinity], Mick Sullivan [St Helens]; Frank Myler [Widnes], Tommy Smales [Huddersfield]; Norman Herbert [Workington Town], Peter Flanagan [Hull Kingston Rovers], Bill Drake [Hull FC], Brian Edgar [Workington Town], Dick Huddart [St Helens] and Derek Turner [Wakefield Trinity]. France, always a different proposition on their own turf, were renowned poor travellers but came tooled up for this one with a big, merciless pack, two clever half backs and some pace in the three quarters. The French team was: Andre Carrere [Lezignan]; Raymond Gruppi [Villeneuve],

Claude Mantoulan [St Gaudens], Bernard Fabre [Albi], Andre Bourreil [Perpignan]; Gilbert Benausse [Lezignan], Louis Verge [Carcassonne]; Aldo Quaglio [Roanne], Georges Llanas [Toulouse], Jean Pano [Villeneuve], Serge Estiau [Roanne], Robert Erramouspe [Roanne] and Georges Fages [Albi]. The referee was Mr Joe Manley of Warrington and the attendance was 11,099.

The afternoon was cold and windy, not at all what the French wanted, as they liked the sun on their backs, with a dry ball to produce those typically French passing moves with the ball coming to hand from impossible angles. Neither could they handle the English pack, with the back three of Brian Edgar, Dick Huddart and Derek Turner in outstanding form. The English had too much pace, size and know-how in the middle backs. Neil Fox was in a particularly belligerent mood with his bulldozing running, and Eric Ashton's long striding runs caused havoc amongst the smaller French backs. Frank had a rare battle at stand off half with the clever Gilbert Benausse who was a tricky customer, but Frank's power and speed off the mark, plus his tough tackling, won him through on the day. France could only muster three goals from the boot of Benausse to give them their six points whilst England ran in four tries and three goals. The speedy Bill Burgess raced in for a brace of tries and Eric Ashton and Neil Fox added one each. Big Neil also added the three goals.

Frank was well satisfied. He had held the tricky Benausse in defence and had given the French stand off a hard time in trying to control Frank's power. Frank's nimble footwork had given him the edge on Gilbert in making Bill Burgess's first try, and a slick dummy and pass had given Neil Fox the chance to get some steam up as he careered over for his three pointer.

Four days after Frank's excellent debut for England, it was time to travel to Central Park, Wigan to replay the Western Competition Final against that uncompromising Cumberland outfit, Workington Town. This time the Cumberland boys proved too much for Widnes and took the new trophy back up to the north west. The 10–0 defeat was a close run thing, with Widnes failing to take a couple of chances that could have given the score line a different look. Widnes were becoming a hard to beat side, and this began to show in their results. The closeness of the scores tells of the resolute determination that Widnes were building. The Leeds home game ended 13–12 and a run of close wins followed: Wakefield Trinity, away, 13–10, Trinity at home, 12–6. One week later, Frank was in Perpignan with the Great Britain side to play France at the Stade Gilbert Brutus. It had been almost two years since Frank's last appearance for Great Britain and he was selected in his favourite spot of stand off half.

The French had won the previous two international games between the countries and figured that the British boys might well be 'short of enthusiasm and rusty' after a hard tour of Australia and New Zealand, ending in August of that year. Great Britain gave seven new caps a debut in this game, Ken Gowers, Bill Burgess, Tommy Smales, Bill Drake, Peter 'Flash' Flanagan, Bill Martin and Ken Bowman. The French pack were dominant from the start as Jean Barthe led from the front to produce a wonderful game against a rather lack lustre British side. Great Britain fielded Ken Gowers [Swinton]; Bill Burgess [Barrow], Eric Ashton [Wigan captain], Neil Fox [Wakefield Trinity], Mick Sullivan [St Helens]; Frank Myler [Widnes], Tommy Smales [Huddersfield]; Bill Drake [Hull FC], Peter Flanagan [Hull Kingston Rovers], Bill Martin [Workington Town], Laurie Gilfedder [Warrington], Ken Bowman [Huddersfield] and Derek Turner [Wakefield Trinity]. France selected Andre Carrere [Lezignan]; Andre Bourreil [Perpignan], Bernard Fabre [Albi], Claude Mantoulan [St Gaudens], Jacques Dubon [Villeneuve]; Gilbert Benausse [Lezignan], Georges Fages [Albi]; Henry Conti [Albi], Andre Vadon [Albi], Aldo Quaglio [Roanne], Robert Eramouspe [Roanne], Jean Barthe [St Gaudens, captain] and Yeves Gourbal [Perpignan]. A crowd of 12,500 attended, and the referee was Monsieur Edouard Martung of Bordeaux.

Going into the final 10 minutes, France were ahead 17–2! The excellent Claude Mantoulan scored a superb try and Gilbert Benausse's two goals were answered only by a Neil Fox penalty goal to put France 7–2 in front at half time. Early in the second half, Benausse and Mantoulan set up a terrific try for Andre Bourreil, then only two minutes later a tremendous Jean Barthe break saw Andre Carrere streak over and, with two further Benausse goals, France had what looked like a match winning lead. Shaking themselves into action the

British found some cheer as Eric Ashton strode over with Neil Fox adding the extra points then Fox himself used his pace and extreme power to crash over and convert his own try. In the final seconds Frank Myler produced a magnificent run which looked all over like a match saving effort. Unfortunately as he rounded Carrere, the French full back, Frank touched the side line with his boot and the score was disallowed! Whilst the result was a magnificent one for France, their tactics included strong arm stuff which went unpunished until the 70th minute when the referee warned the two captains. The officials ignored the high shots and punches, and this drew a harsh reprimand from the British manager Mr Bill Fallowfield who stated that 'Britain were 20 points better than the French but were not allowed to play'.

It was back to the exacting but rewarding weekly cycle of league fixtures at Widnes, but the scope of the toughness of immediate games came as a shock to all Naughton Park players. Already having played some close and hard games such as Hull Kingston Rovers away, 15–12, Oldham at home 3–0, Hull Kingston Rovers at home 9–7, there was an even harder era awaiting Widnes. Then came an unbelievably brutal spell of games starting with Swinton away in the Challenge Cup on 6 March. This game ended at 6 points all. Three days later Widnes played Hull FC and won 15–10. Two days later came the replay at Naughton Park against Swinton and this game ended 3 points all. Two days went by and again Widnes and Swinton met at Wigan in the second replay. This result was another nail biter with Widnes winning 6–4. Three days later on Saturday, Widnes played Whitehaven at Widnes in the second round of the Challenge Cup and won 5–nil! These were strength sapping matches and on top of them came an 8–3 defeat at Oldham, a 10–7 defeat by Hull Kingston Rovers in the third round of the Challenge Cup then yet another draw against Featherstone Rovers, 11 points each. Including the Lancashire Cup game, Widnes played Swinton six times in the season. The final 11 games of the season gave Widnes six wins and five losses.

It had been an exhausting season. Drawing games in cup ties put great pressure on the players as they had to face replays. But Frank finished the season with 12 tries for the club and again found that playing alongside his cousin, Vince Karalius, gave not only Frank, but all the side, extra confidence.

7

A LONG, HARD ROAD TO WEMBLEY

Off the field, 1963 proved a happy time for Frank and Eileen as their first child Greg was born. On the field however, the 1963–64 season proved a hard one for both Widnes and Frank. The team played 51 games in this term including the unusually high number of six drawn games, five having to be replayed. The Western Competition was continued, as it had proved a good 'stocking filler' to the shortened season caused by the reintroduction of the two division system. It provided an extra eight games and there was a fixture against the touring Australians. Widnes again played Swinton six times in this season in games stretching from the league, Western Competition and two draws and two replays in the Challenge Cup.

Of the 51 games played, Frank figured in the centre for 21 of them, and in his favoured stand off spot for another 20. Frank crossed the line for tries on seven occasions in his 41 games. The league season began with a satisfactory five wins out of the first eight games, and the County Championship started again on 11 September 1963 with a game against Yorkshire at Knowsley Road, St Helens. Lancashire fancied their chances of winning the inter-county shield and selected a strong side to open the Championship fixture. Ken Gowers [Swinton]; Bill Burgess [Barrow], Keith Northey [St Helens], Alan Buckley [Swinton], Jonnny Stopford [Swinton]; Frank Myler [Widnes], Alex Murphy [St Helens]; Bill Robinson [Leigh], Bill Sayer [Wigan], Edgar Bate [Widnes], Jim Measures [Widnes], Laurie Gilfedder

[Wigan] and Vince Karalius [Widnes]. Yorkshire were also at strength and fielded Frank Dyson [Oldham]; Gary Waterworth [Featherstone Rovers], Geoff Shelton [Hunslet], Terry Major [Hull Kingston Rovers], Norman Field [Batley]; Brian Wrigglesworth [Bramley], Dave Elliott [Hull Kingston Rovers]; Jack Hirst [Castleford], Peter Flanagan [Hull Kingston Rovers], Brian Tyson [Hull Kingston Rovers], Ron Morgan [Swinton], Ken Bowman [Huddersfield] and Fred Ward [Hunslet]. The referee was that upright fellow, Mr Eric Clay of Rothwell and the gate was 11,200.

Playing brilliant football, Lancashire took Yorkshire to the cleaners with a 45–20 win. In the nine try romp, Jim Measures scored three tries, Alex Murphy two and Bill Burgess, Alan Buckley, Johnny Stopford and Vince Karalius a try apiece, with Laurie Gilfedder kicking nine goals. Yorkshire replied with Norman Field, Jack Hirst, Ron Morgan and Fred Ward scoring tries, and Frank Dyson kicking four goals. Frank recalls this particular game: 'Our pack were on top of the Yorkshire forwards from the word go. Alex Murphy was in great form too, but our man of the match was Jim Measures whose speed on the run was amazing. His support play was top class, as his pace allowed him to keep close to the backs making breaks. Our pack was led magnificently by Vince Karalius whose ball handling around the edges of the Yorkshire defence was outstanding. Bill Robinson and Edgar Bate grafted throughout the whole game and Bill Sayer did his usual strong tackling stint and won us a load of ball from the scrums. Laurie Gilfedder made some telling breaks as well as kicking his nine goals.'

This win put Lancashire on track to lift the County Championship if they could beat the strong Cumberland side at Whitehaven the following month. This was easier said than done as the Cumberland side were particularly hard to beat on their own soil. Frank knew that the Lancashire pack would have it much tougher up in Whitehaven than they had at St Helens. Frank missed 10 Widnes games through knocks, bumps and injuries that occur in a run of the mill season, playing 51 games! Frank's comment about this was, 'The club were lucky to have good, keen young players to step in and play in almost every position, and sometimes it was hard getting your place back if you had received an injury. My longest time out of the side was a six game miss from 16 November 1963 to 26 December 1963 as well as the odd game now and again towards the end of the season.'

No one at Widnes knew what was around the corner, as the season headed towards the Challenge Cup games. One of the games Frank missed was the Widnes v Australian tourists' game played on 21 November. The Aussies were too good for Widnes who put up a brave fight to be beaten 20–9 before a crowd of 6,602. Frank returned at stand off on 26 December for the game against Warrington at home but Widnes lost this traditionally hard-fought 'derby', 16–7.

Two days later Widnes travelled to Hunslet to take on the hardnosed players from South Leeds. Hunslet were in a rich seam of form, claiming a double over Leeds, home and away that season. The Hunslet team was Billy Langton; John Griffiths, Geoff Shelton, Alan Preece, Tommy Thompson; Brian Gabbitas, Jeff Stevenson; Denis Hartley, Bernard Prior, Kenny Eyre, Billy Baldwinson, Geoff Gunney and Fred Ward. Widnes relied on Bob Randall; Johnny Gaydon, Alan Briers, Ged Lowe, Derek Heyes; Frank Myler, Ray Owen; Wally Hurstfield, George Kemel, Alan Walsh, Brian Winstanley, Arthur Hughes and Vince Karalius. Hunslet won the game 9–0.

This season the Widnes Western Competition opponents were Leigh, Rochdale Hornets, Liverpool City and Salford. These matches were spread throughout the league fixtures, the first game in early October 1963, and the semi final just seven days before the Wembley final in May 1964. Widnes managed to reach the Western Competition semi final, but it was mostly thanks to other clubs beating the sides that beat Widnes in the competition. The results in the Western Competition went, Leigh, home, won 20–0, Leigh, away, lost 14–3. Rochdale Hornets, home, won 17–9, Rochdale Hornets, away, drew 7 points all. Liverpool City, home, won 10–9, Liverpool City, away, won 18–10. Salford, home, won 11–10, Salford, away, won 15–9.

These results took Widnes into the semi final of the Western Competition against Swinton at Station Road on 2 May 1964. With another match the week after on their minds, Widnes lost the semi 21–5. In league football, Widnes had certainly enjoyed more successful campaigns as their record showed played 30, won 13, lost 17. The full playing record of the whole season was played 51 matches, won 24, lost 21, drawn 6, but these included playing the touring Australians, the Western Competition, the Lancashire Cup and the Challenge Cup. Widnes had come out of the Lancashire Cup in the first round defeat away to Oldham and Frank remembers this extra hard season:

> Playing 30 odd league games was strenuous enough but with all the draws and replays plus the extended Western Competition, this was a long, hard season indeed. Our Challenge Cup run that season would normally have meant playing five games to get through to Wembley. In our case it took 10 games as we drew five games in the run! The board came up with a great signing for us prior to the game on 25 January 1964 when they splashed out for Frank Collier the big Wigan forward and brought him to Naughton Park just in time for the cup ties. Frank was already an international forward and he gave our pack a rosy look when playing alongside Vince and company. Frank was an excellent prop or second rower and a comedian both on and off the field, great in the dressing room and he made his presence felt on his debut for Widnes in the tough environment of the Boulevard against Hull FC in our 13–8 win.

Widnes did have some good league results beating Wakefield Trinity at Naughton Park 7–3, Leeds were defeated home and away, 26–6 at Headingley and 27–9 at home, St Helens away 10–6 and Swinton in the Challenge Cup by 15–3. In fact, as stated previously, Widnes played Swinton six times in this season but beat them only once.

On the Lancashire County scene, the great result against Yorkshire at St Helens filled the committee with confidence. The Red Rose side had a fixture against the touring Australians at Wigan on 25 September. The Aussies, who would go on to win the Ashes Cup with a two Tests to one win, had already lost to Yorkshire at Craven Park, Hull Kingston Rovers' ground 11–5 before a crowd of 10,324, so the Lancashire lads expected a backlash.

Lancashire made three changes for this game against the Aussies, Trevor Simms of Oldham came in on the wing for Bill Burgess, Graham Williams of Swinton was at half back for Alex Murphy and Roy Evans of Wigan came into the second row for Laurie Gilfedder. The team was Ken Gowers [Swinton]; Trevor Simms [Oldham], Keith Northey [Saints], Alan Buckley [Swinton], Johnny Stopford [Swinton]; Frank Myler [Widnes], Graham Williams [Swinton]; Bill Robinson [Leigh], Bill Sayer [Wigan], Edgar Bate [Widnes], Jim Measures [Widnes], Roy Evans [Wigan] and Vince Karalius [Widnes]. The one substitute was George Parkinson [Swinton] who replaced Ken Gowers during the game. The Aussies, who were keen to take revenge over the defeat by Yorkshire, selected Les Johns [Canterbury Bankstown]; Ken Irvine [North Sydney], Graeme Langlands [St George], Barry Rushworth [Lithgow], Mike Cleary [South Sydney]; Earl Harrison [Gilgandra], Barry Muir [West Brisbane]; Peter Gallagher [Brisbane Brothers], Ian Walsh [St George], Noel Kelly [Western Suburbs], Dick Thornett [Parramatta], Brian Hambly [Parramatta] and Johnny Raper [St George]. This was a big, physical team containing some excellent Test-class backs. The referee for this almost Test level game was Mr Matt Coates of Pudsey, and the gate was a healthy 15,068.

The Australians laid down the ground rules early on, with hard man Noel Kelly introducing himself to one or two of the Lancashire forwards. It was a real tussle with players from both sides defending themselves from attacks on the run. A break by Frank and quick support by Jim Measures saw the speedy forward race over to draw first blood. Then Graham Williams shot away from a close in scrum and dived over for a well taken try. Moving the ball wide to use the pace of Ken Irvine and Mike Cleary, Barry Rushworth had the tall Mike Cleary speeding along the touchline and stepping inside the desperate lunge of Ken Gowers to register a grand try. Ian Walsh dummied his way over for a try from a play the ball near the home line, with Les Johns converting to give the Aussies an 8–6 lead. Two goals for Lancashire by Ken Gowers and Keith Northey gave the lead back to Lancashire, before Dick Thornett crashed over to give Australia what appeared to be the match winning score. But superb handling by

Lancashire's backs gave the fast moving Trevor Simms a slight opening on the side line and his pace was too much for the covering Les Johns as the Oldham flyer dashed in by the corner flag. The whistle blew to end a terrific game with Lancashire the 13–11 winners.

Seven days later came the County Championship decider up in Whitehaven, as both Lancashire and Cumberland had beaten Yorkshire. Wholesale changes were unlikely by the Lancashire committee for the trek up to Cumberland. The magnificent win against Australia only seven days earlier was fresh in the minds of the selectors for this vital inter-county game. Three changes were made for injured players meaning Ray Ashby came in for Ken Gowers at full back, Peter Harvey was in on the wing for Johnny Stopford and Laurie Gilfedder returned as the goal kicker for Roy Evans. Cumberland saw this as a great opportunity to snatch the County Championship as they too had beaten Yorkshire in the earlier round. The side selected by the Cumberland committee was a typical no nonsense one, as followers of the game would expect from these hard men from the north west. It was Syd Lowden [Workington Town]; Louis Shepherd [Whitehaven], John O'Neil [Workington Town], Eric Bell [Workington Town], Tony Colloby [Whitehaven]; Harry Archer [Workington Town], Sol Roper [Workington Town]; Brian Edgar [Workington Town], Jim Lynch [Whitehaven], John Temby [St Helens], Dick Huddart [Workington Town], Frank Foster [Workington Town] and Derek Hurt [Leigh]. A decent 6,000-strong crowd eagerly read their programmes to see who would be facing their heroes. Lancashire went for Ray Ashby [Liverpool City]; Trevor Simms [Oldham], Keith Northey [St Helens], Alan Buckley [Swinton], Peter Harvey [St Helens]; Frank Myler [Widnes], Graham Williams [Swinton]; Bill Robinson [Leigh], Bill Sayer [Wigan], Edgar Bate [Widnes], Jim Measures [Widnes], Laurie Gilfedder [Wigan] and Vince Karalius [Widnes]. Cumberland v Lancashire had the reputation for being challenging matches. This tie was no different.

From the start the Cumberland pack took the game to their southern opponents. Brian Edgar and Frank Foster led the charge with able support from Derek Hurt, Jim Lynch, Dick Huddart and John

St Bedes under 11s rugby team photo

Widnes v Halifax (Challenge Cup 1956). Harry Dawson and Geoff Palmer vie for the ball (I'm in the background bringing up the rear)

Great Britain 1960 World Cup team at Leeds RLFC Headingley

Widnes v Workington, 1962 Western Division Final at Wigan

Widnes v Hull Kingston Rovers

Lifting the Challenge Cup at Wembley

Amongst the pigeons at Trafalgar Square with Eileen, Vin, Barbara and the cup

Widnes 1964 Challenge Cup winners (I'm on the row directly behind the cup, third from the right)

Posing with the cup in Trafalgar Square after the 1964 final with Mr and Mrs Begley, Mary and Bill Tompson, Vin and Barbara Karalius and Eileen

Our wedding day—the service was conducted by my mum's cousin Fr Vincent Karalius

Greg, Eileen, Chris and Denise, 1970

1965 GB v France at Swinton

1966 Lions squad taken at Leeds RLFC, Headingley

In action at Central Park, St Helens

Temby. Frank recalls the game:

> I played in some brutal inter-county games but this one was just about the hardest. The ground at Whitehaven was most unusual in that the crowd seemed to be on the field with you because they were so close to the on-field action. Dick Huddart was his usual dangerous self with his powerful and speedy wide running. My immediate opponent was the strong running Harry Archer. Harry and I had played against each other on many occasions and his style never altered. Very powerful in build, his pace was good and his evasive qualities were excellent. He possessed a strong hand off and this could be lethal if a tackle was not in the perfect place. We had a real hard game against each other, but as always Harry was first to shake hands after the final whistle. Big Frank Foster was a handful, strong and aggressive, and he and Derek Hurt enforced the hard style play that the Cumberland boys produced. As the game progressed it developed into a kind of hard cup tie and the result hinged on the final try and two drop goals. It was a very close run thing and there was no doubt that the almost fanatical support that the Cumberland boys received from those tremendous Cumbrian fans helped swing the game to them.

Cumberland took the County Championship with a fine 13–8 win. Their try scorers were Louis Shepherd, John O'Neil and Dick Huddart, with Frank Foster, of all people, landing two goals. Huddart's try was a typical long range effort worthy of winning any game. Vince Karalius, a big pal for years of Dick Huddart, was a tower of strength for Lancashire and had a storming game. Their eight points came in the shape of tries by Trevor Simms and Edgar Bate with Laurie Gilfedder landing one goal. So Cumberland lifted the County Championship and their players were awarded the beautiful gold medal for their endeavours. The Lancashire players were as disappointed as the County Committee. They had come so close to lifting the trophy but the fighting spirit of the Cumberland side held together and this saw them through.

February came around and with it came the draw for the first round of the old Challenge Cup. The first round date was 8 February but on the first day of the month Widnes played Castleford at Naughton Park and a good 16–10 win for Widnes boosted the team's confidence. In the Challenge Cup draw, Widnes drew a hard first round trip to Leigh. Hilton Park was a difficult place to win at. Leigh played a brand of football that suited them and they could score a hat full of points should the opposition fail to defend stoutly. Their pack contained some of the better county players such as Bill Robinson, Mick Martyn of Lancashire and Derek Hurt of Cumberland. Their backs had pace and they were a dangerous outfit.

True to form, this first round tie was a gruelling, iron clad defence orientated battle. Despite both sides' feverish attempts to cross their opponents' try line, the game ended in a 2 points all draw before a crowd of just over 10,000. Frank recalls, 'This was a typical hard fought cup tie with tactics built around defence by both sides. The two packs of forwards cancelled each other out with ferocious tackling and scoring was reduced to one goal apiece.'

Widnes ace kicker Randall landed one and Colin Tyrer replied in similar vein for Leigh. The Widnes team on duty for this first round tie was Robin Whitfield; Johnny Gaydon, Alan Briers, Bill Thompson, Bob Randall; Frank Myler, Ray Owen; Edgar Bate, Tony Karalius, Alan Walsh, Frank Collier, Jim Measures and Arthur Hughes. The replay at Naughton Park was on Wednesday 12 February when a similar attendance of 9,800 witnessed another gigantic struggle. This time more points were registered in another draw, this time an 11 points affair. Leigh's try scorers were Bev Risman, Mick Collins and Tony Leadbetter with Tyrer landing one goal. The Widnes scorers were Jim Measures with a try, and Bob Randall kicked four goals. 'Leigh played really well,' said Frank, 'and it gives some idea just how well they played as they scored three tries to our one. But it was an enthralling game with excitement throughout as neither team could break away from the other's grasp.'

The Widnes side remained the same in the replay as they had in the first game. Finally the whistle sounded to end the game sending the two teams into a third game decider. This was played at Knowsley Road, St Helens on Monday 17 February. Between the second and third Leigh games, Widnes had to play a fixture away against Salford in the Western Competition which they won 15–9. The second replay against Leigh drew in a grand crowd of 12,500.

Widnes finally overcame another fierce encounter against Leigh with a winning score of 14–2. This time the Widnes forwards dominated the Leigh pack, and tries by Jim Measures and Arthur Hughes and another four goals by Bob Randall pointed the way towards another hard game, the second round tie against Liverpool City at home. In the second replay Widnes made some changes to their side. Randall moved off the wing to replace Whitfield at full back, Frank moved from stand off to centre for Thompson and Chisnall filled in for Randall. Ged Lowe came in at stand off and the reshaped pack read Hurstfield, Kemel, Edgar Bate, Collier, Measures and Hughes. Widnes beat Liverpool City 16–6 in another hard fought game. Vince Karalius had not played for five games and his presence had been missed in the Leigh trilogy. He returned for the home league game against Keighley, won 26–15 and was declared fit to play the following week against Liverpool in the cup tie. Swinton had been drawn to play Widnes in the Challenge Cup third round at Naughton Park but a confidence sapping defeat away at the hands of Workington Town by 21–0 in a league game prior to the Swinton cup tie made for an uncomfortable week to wait for the Lions.

Swinton had a very good side in the early to middle 1960s with excellent players in both backs and forwards. Top players for Swinton were Ken Gowers at full back, Alan Buckley in the centre, Johnny Stopford on the wing and two excellent half backs in George Parkinson and Albert Cartwright. Future international star, Dave Robinson was loose forward. Widnes met fire with fire, and put out a strong looking team, Bob Randall; Johnny Gaydon, Alan Briers, Frank Myler, Bobby Chisnall; Ged Lowe, Ray Owen; Wally Hurstfield, George Kemel, Edgar Bate, Frank Collier, Jim Measures and Vince Karalius. Two titanic struggles took place in the following five days between these two evenly matched teams. The first game on 14 March ended in a 5 points all draw, the second, an even more battle royal, finished at 0–0. After 160 minutes of football only 10 points were scored. Frank remembers, 'The first game at Widnes was one we should possibly have won but water tight defence and a superb display by our pack pulled us through. The experience and determination of Vince, Frank Collier, Jim Measures, Edgar Bate, George Kemel and Wally Hurstfield was a blueprint of how not to lose a cup tie. They were magnificent!'

The replay at Station Road Swinton was even closer. Try as both sides might they could not breach each other's iron defences. They showed discipline and neither side had much chance of kicking any penalty points due to will power and instructions from both coaches about not giving away penalty kicks. It was on to another second replay, but this time at Central Park, Wigan, on Monday 23 March. On Saturday 21 March, Widnes beat Liverpool City in the Western Competition at Naughton Park by 10–9! Widnes had played 12 games in 49 days, one exhausting game every four days! Playing so many hard fixtures with little time to recover didn't seem to weaken the Widnes resolve, but rather to inspire them.

Central Park was in great shape for the second replay, and this suited Widnes who showed few features of fatigue as they came out shooting from the hip. Both sides made changes as the ferocity of these competitive games took their toll on one or two players. The Widnes side was Randall; Gaydon, Frank Myler, Thompson, Chisnall; Lowe, Owen; Hurstfield, Kemel, Edgar Bate, Hughes, Measures and Vince Karalius. Tries by Johnny Gaydon, Frank Myler and Bill Thompson and three Bob Randall goals saw Widnes to a 15–3 win as they moved along in this cup run to the semi final and a match against the strong Yorkshire outfit, Castleford. But there were five tough games to play before the semi final of the cup. Widnes had to face Western Competition opposition in the form of Salford and Rochdale Hornets at home and in the league, Warrington, St Helens and, would you believe, Swinton, all away.

Widnes accounted for Salford in an 11–10 win and Rochdale in a 17–9 victory. The stronger Warrington side scored a resounding 29–10 win over Widnes and another visit to Station Road, Swinton, just one week before the big game against Castleford, brought revenge to the Lions as they beat a Widnes side, minus Frank Myler, by 22–6. The game wedged in between Warrington and Swinton was the intimidating visit to Knowsley Road to take on the mighty Saints. It was Saturday 4 April, and St Helens were as strong as they could be. Their team sheet read Keith Northey; Tom van Vollenhoven, Ken Williams, Bryan Todd, Len Killeen; Wilf Smith, Billy Benyon; John Temby, Bob Burdell, John Warlow, Ray French, Mervyn Hicks and Doug Laughton. Widnes fielded Whitfield; Gaydon, Frank Myler, Thompson, Chisnall; Lowe, Owen; Ronnie Bate, Tony Karalius, Walsh, Measures, Hughes and Vince Karalius.

Playing some great football and tackling like demons, Widnes shocked even their own faithful supporters with a vintage performance to come away from Knowsley Road with a fine 10–6 victory. Jim Measures and Arthur Hughes scored tries and Robin Whitfield kicked two goals against two St Helens tries by Keith Northey and Mervyn Hicks.

So onto the semi final against Castleford whose form over the recent seasons found them maturing into a very good side, similar to Widnes in that the team was full to the brim of local lads who played a great deal for the club itself. They played the game at Station Road, Swinton and attracted a crowd of 25,603. Widnes were at strength and fielded Randall; Gaydon, Briers, Frank Myler, Chisnall; Lowe, Owen; Hurstfield, Kemel, Edgar Bate, Collier, Measures and Vince Karalius. Frank remembers the game vividly, 'It was a very difficult game. A real struggle. Castleford boasted plenty of good youngsters who had a great pride in their club. Big Bill Bryant in their second row, Jack Hirst at prop, Alan Hardisty and Keith Hepworth at half back all contributed to a hard performance in that semi final'. The game was so hard and fierce that the final score at Swinton was 7 points all. It was yet another draw for Widnes. Frank scored a super try in this semi final and Randall kicked two goals.

Strangely, over at Headingley one week earlier the other two semi finalists, Hull Kingston Rovers and Oldham, had been involved in a dour struggle ending in another draw at 5 points all. Both replays took place on the following Wednesday's. The Hull Kingston Rovers v Oldham game was played at Swinton, and the Widnes v Castleford replay took place at Belle Vue, Wakefield before a crowd of 28,739.

Another titanic battle was fought out as Widnes made one change from the previous game, Thompson taking the place of the injured Gaydon on the wing. This time the replacement Thompson sped over for the Widnes try and Randall again contributed two goals in Widnes's 7–5 nail biting win! Frank commented, 'At last we were there at Wembley! The directors were delighted and the players were ecstatic! Widnes had played in four previous Wembley Challenge Cup finals, winning two and losing two but this was the first time for the vast majority of our players'. Vince and Frank Collier had played on the big ground at Wembley several times and both offered advice about various aspects of the ground, the huge crowd, and urged us to soak up the atmosphere of this brilliant occasion 'as you may only ever get one chance to play there'.

Widnes's opponents in the final found reaching Wembley more difficult than Widnes. Their semi final replay was held at Swinton and after 80 minutes the score was 14 points all. They were forced to play extra time as a winning result was crucial on the night. This was because time was running out with only 24 days left before the Wembley final. (The league games were piling up with, for example, Widnes having to play three games in 10 days from the semi final replay on 22 April to 2 May, one week before the cup final.) Then in the Hull Kingston Rovers v Oldham game, after 12 minutes of extra time and with Oldham winning 17–14, it became dark. Because there were no floodlights on the ground, the referee abandoned the game and a second replay was arranged at Huddersfield's Fartown ground. The decision was particularly harsh on the loyal Oldham supporters as their team was in front when the game was abandoned. Despite this they still had to replay the game. At Fartown, Hull Kingston Rovers did most things right and beat unlucky Oldham 12–2. In the five semi finals of this competition, 139,097 spectators watched the games bringing £30,377 through the gate, a substantial sum in those days.

So the Challenge Cup final of the 1963–64 season at Wembley was fought out between Widnes and Hull Kingston Rovers. When Frank looks back on that epic season, and the Challenge Cup in particular, his comments are profound: 'Widnes certainly did it the hard way that season. If one looks at the normal passage to Wembley, the team winning the cup goes on a five game winning run. At Widnes we played nine games to reach the final and that included five draws. It was indeed a hard road, and I doubt if any other team has ever taken such a difficult path to the Challenge Cup final.'

Between the Castleford replay and the Wembley final, Widnes had three games to play. Two of these games, St Helens at home and Wakefield Trinity away, were in the league, and one, Swinton away, was in the Western Competition. Widnes lost all three games as the predominant thought was naturally on the big game at Wembley on 9 May. Frank was in the centre against Saints, missed the Wakefield Trinity game but was back at stand off half for the visit by Swinton to Naughton Park. The results of the three games were Saints 19–8, Wakefield Trinity 20–10 and Swinton 21–5. Obviously selections were made to allow rests for some of the key players in these games as the big day was not too far away.

The team that played Saints on Saturday, three days after the Castleford replay was Bob Randall; Bobby Chisnall, Alan Briers, Frank Myler, Bill Thompson; Alan Willacy, Ged Smith; Wally Hurstfield, George Kemel, Edgar Bate, Ronnie Bate, Ken Parton and Jim Measures. Then on the following Wednesday at Wakefield an almost unrecognisable Widnes team was Robin Whitfield; Johnny Gaydon, Briers, Thompson, Derek Heyes; Willacy, G. Smith; Ronnie Bate, Tony Karalius, Eric Lines, Alan Walsh, Brian Winstanley and Parton. In the final game before Wembley the team which played against Swinton in the Western Competition was Randall; Gaydon, Briers, Thompson, Chisnall; Frank Myler, Ray Owen; Hurstfield, Kemel, Edgar Bate, Measures, Frank Collier and Arthur Hughes. All was set for the great Wembley experience.

8

HULL KINGSTON ROVERS AT WEMBLEY

The talking was over and a tap on the dressing room door told the players and coaching staff that it was time for action. The players remembered that Hull Kingston Rovers had knocked them out of the Challenge Cup last season with a rousing 10–7 win at Naughton Park, so the Widnes boys knew just how dangerous a side they were.

Edgar Bate was the experienced and desperately unfortunate Widnes player who was left out of the cup final side after playing in 30 of the 42 preceding games and despite being an almost ever-present in the front row for quite a few seasons. It was a shock decision and the supporters felt for the long serving prop. All the players were saddened by the omission of Edgar from the team. Frank Collier, who had already played twice for Wigan at Wembley and had two Wembley medals, offered to stand down and let Edgar take his place. Despite his disappointment at not being selected, Edgar, being the sportsman that he was, refused Collier's offer. He realised that the reason he hadn't been selected was to balance the pack. Frank says, 'I was sad for Edgar as we had both been playing consistently for Widnes since our first game together and we had been friends for a long time. He was one of the most underrated players of his day. He was tenacious. I have never seen before or since a fellow of his stature who could tackle so well, he was over 6ft tall and weighed 16 stone. He had a knack of tackling taking both feet, he wasn't taking people's heads off. He had his own unique style and I can't think of a player who could time a tackle so well.'

Frank was selected in the centre with Ged Lowe at stand off. The team on duty for Widnes was Bob Randall; Bobby Chisnall, Alan Briers, Frank Myler, Bill Thompson; Ged Lowe, Ray Owen; Wally Hurstfield, George Kemel, Frank Collier, Jim Measures, Arthur Hughes and Vince Karalius. The Hull Kingston Rovers team were missing suspended prop John Taylor and, with that grand grafting forward Jim Drake also injured, his place was taken by the youngster, Brian Mennell. The Rovers team was, Cyril Kellett; Graham Paul, Terry Major, David Elliott, Mike Blackmore; Alan Burwell, Arthur Bunting; Brian Tyson, Peter Flanagan, Brian Mennell, Eric Palmer, Len Clark and Harry Poole.

The teams representing Widnes and Hull Kingston Rovers strode out of the Wembley tunnel, side by side, onto the famed turf with immense pride on 9 May 1964. They were greeted by a cheering crowd of 84,488. The dignitaries presented to the teams that year were his Royal Highness The Duke of Edinburgh, Prince Philip and Lord Derby, Rugby League president. Now Vince Karalius was the club captain and he warned his players about acting the fool in front of the Royal Prince. Vince's biggest threat came from the natural comic, big Frank Collier, and Vince quietly told Frank that there must be no monkey business out there on the pitch whilst being presented to His Highness.

The teams lined up in the usual pose, Hull Kingston Rovers in their all red jerseys instead of their usual all white strip with the single broad vivid red band across the chest, hence their nickname 'The Robins'. Widnes looked a smart set with their brand new black and white hooped jerseys and spotless white shorts. In those days the captain was introduced to the celebrity by the club Chairman, and then the captain accompanied the celebrity down the line of his players introducing each one individually. Vince anxiously looked down the line to see if big Frank was behaving himself and, apart from the odd little glance towards the Duke, all seemed fine. Finally the VIP party arrived at big Frank and Vince duly introduced the Duke to him, 'And this, sir, is Frank Collier. He recently joined us from the Wigan club,' said Vince as Frank looked on in a picture of innocence.

The Duke offered his hand in the usual royal way, very light and gentle. Frank grabbed the Duke's hand and shook it in a good hearted way saying, 'Hello Your Highness, how's the wife and kids?' Big Frank, with his good natured friendliness and his cheek, helped to ease the Widnes tension before the kick off.

Hull Kingston Rovers were a very good side. Their half backs, Alan Burwell and Arthur Bunting were in excellent form having had a particularly good season. Cyril Kellett at full back was an outstanding goal kicker and a resolute defender. In their three quarters they boasted a quick, skilful and strong back division which included two excellent wingmen in Graham Paul and Mike Blackmore. Paul, the 'Cornish Express' was particularly rapid with good evasive qualities. The Robins pack, although lacking the experience and no nonsense go-forward running of John Taylor, were big and mobile with the three key figures of Brian Tyson at prop, Peter 'Flash' Flanagan at hooker and their skipper Harry Poole at loose forward. The players were expected to be a dangerous trio facing the Widnes boys.

Widnes needed their star men to perform well and looked to teamwork, team spirit and that vital touch of excellent play from the likes of Frank Myler, Vince Karalius and Frank Collier to support their first class defence. All the Widnes key players turned out great games for the club just when it was required. Vince broke the early deadlock with a superb break and pass to the supporting Alan Briers who zoomed over for a very good try. A typical Frank Myler try, all pace and power, followed, and there was no stopping the big Frank Collier near the Hull Kingston Rovers line. He forced his way over to give the Chemics three excellent tries to go with two Bob Randall goals giving the men in black and white the Challenge Cup with a score of Widnes 13 Hull Kingston Rovers 5.

The Widnes supporters were ecstatic with joy as their champions paraded the glorious old cup around the stadium. There were several candidates for the coveted Lance Todd Trophy for the best and fairest player of the final, but in the end it went to Frank Collier for his nonstop work rate, and, of course, his try helped enormously. Widnes celebrated in the dressing room, and everyone was in great humour. After a celebratory dinner at The Waldorf Hotel some of the players and their wives took the team bus and drove to Euston Station with the cup. They knew that there would still be a large number of Widnes fans waiting to board the train back to Widnes, and they wanted to thank them for their support. They were given an ecstatic welcome when they arrived on the platform carrying the cup. Widnes's win at Wembley and the fighting spirit shown by the team in the march to the Twin Towers, laid a foundation for the later Widnes teams. Two decades into the future Widnes players earned their own notoriety as well as the nickname The Cup Kings through some outstanding cup wins.

All involved in the historic homecoming for the heroes of Wembley in 1964 will remember it. Thousands of supporters lined the route as the team showed off the old Challenge Cup to the Widnes adoring public. Frank remembers;

> It was a remarkable occasion. There were thousands upon thousands of people, senior citizens, middle aged couples, young couples, children, babies, all cheering and waving black and white scarves and flags. It was outstanding. All the players were involved in the festivities, with Frank Collier the life and soul of the party. Everyone wanted to touch the cup for luck, everyone was happy and singing and cheering. We were honoured by a Town Hall reception and no one believed that so many people could live in Widnes. Supporters must have come into town from miles around. It was great being a local lad to see such support for the team.

The Widnes club had played in a massive 51 games in that cup winning season. Frank played in 41 of those games as both a centre and a stand off half proving again that he was a tremendous club man. His outstanding qualities also earned him selection in these two positions for Lancashire County and the Great Britain national side and took him on two Lions tours, 1966 and 1970 as captain, to Australia and New Zealand. The two defeats in the final three games of that historic season didn't really matter as holding the Challenge Cup for 12 months was more important.

So with the great cup run in mind, Widnes and Frank approached the 1964–65 season in good heart. But it was to be a disappointing season, with Widnes winning only 14 of the 34 league games and drawing two, Leigh at home 2–2 and Halifax away 5–5. Another draw occurred in early February with a mammoth 2 points all at Naughton Park against the tough Workington Town in the first round Challenge Cup tie. In the replay at Derwent Park, Widnes lost the game against Workington in another unbelievably hard encounter by 2–0! Widnes had also been bundled out of the Lancashire Cup by Swinton at Station Road by 11–7 earlier in the season. Losing 18 games in the league, and finishing 19th of the 30 clubs, Widnes took part in the short lived 'Bottom 14' competition games at the end of the season and beat the reformed Bradford Northern at home 15–9 only to be beaten the following week by Huddersfield at Fartown by 15–12. Frank had played in 26 games, 14 in the centre and 12 at stand off. So after the euphoric Wembley season came this less than satisfactory term.

One good point about this disappointing season was that Frank maintained his international standing with the Great Britain selectors. The regular game against France was imminent and the letter from rugby league HQ arrived informing Frank that he had been selected for the first cross channel Test in December 1964. The game was to be played at the Gilbert Brutus Stadium in Perpignan. Frank had made his international debut in the 1960 World Cup game against the Kiwis at Odsal and had played against the French five times before.

9

BACK TO INTERNATIONAL AND COUNTY FOOTBALL

Frank had been out of international football since damaging his ribs in the Test against Australia on 9 November 1963 at Swinton in the heavy 50–12 defeat. His recall was not at stand off but in the centre to partner the Welsh sprinter Berwyn Jones. The Great Britain side that afternoon was Ken Gowers [Swinton]; Berwyn Jones [Wakefield Trinity], Frank Myler [Widnes], Dick Gemmell [Leeds], Johnny Stopford [Swinton]; Alan Hardisty [Castleford], Alex Murphy [St Helens, captain]; John Warlow [St Helens], Bob Dagnall [St Helens], John Tembey [St Helens], Geoff Gunney [Hunslet], Bill Holliday [Whitehaven] and Harry Poole [Hull Kingston Rovers].

France returned from a disastrous tour of Australia and New Zealand at the start of the European competition and faced losing all six Test matches against the Aussies and Kiwis. The British selectors went into this game with five international debutants as the thinking was that the French would be shell shocked from the mauling 'down under'. But having a great lead from their two key forwards, captain Marcel Bescos and the excellent Georges Ailleres, they showed little after effects of the exacting tour. The French side was Pierre Lacaze [Toulouse]; Guy Bruzy [Perpignan], Jean-Pierre Lecompton [St Gaudens], Gerard Savonne [Marseille], Andre Ferran [Avignon]; Etienne Courtine [Villeneuve], Roger Garnung [Bordeaux]; Jean Pano [Villeneuve], Rene Segura [Carcassonne], Marcel Bescos [Limoux captain], Henri Marracq [St Gaudens], Georges Ailleres [Toulouse] and Yvon Gourbal [Perpignan]. The referee was one of France's best, Monsieur Georges Jameau of Marseille.

The French won the game 18–8 but both sides scored two tries each and only Pierre Lacaze's expert goal kicking (he landed four) and Etienne Courtine (who managed to drop two superb goals) gave the French their 10 points margin. Britain's two tries came from a typical piece of terrific support play from Alan Hardisty who accepted John Tembey's slick pass to race in from 40 yards. Frank Myler had a big hand in the other Great Britain try as he sent sprinter Berwyn Jones away on the half way line. The former Olympic 100 metres finalist displayed fantastic pace to beat several French coverers. As he zoomed down the touchline the French crowd chanted 'Le Rapide!' But the goal kicker for Great Britain had an off day and the powerful Guy Bruzy crashed over for two tries that swung the game to France and they deserved their win.

Frank had to miss the tough home 2–2 draw in the Widnes v Leigh league game at Naughton Park because of the trip to Perpignan. He also missed the home game against Halifax as he was playing France in the return game at Swinton on 23 January 1965. The Halifax game ended in 12–3 a win for Widnes. The harsh battle in the league is illustrated by the Widnes results in the months of December 1964 and January 1965. In December came a 2-all draw with Leigh, a 15–5 defeat against Barrow and a hard fought 22–15 win over Blackpool Borough. In January was a 13–0 win against Whitehaven, a 5-all draw against Halifax then the following week came a 12–3 win over Halifax and a 16–10 victory against Salford. All were hard close games.

The return game against France at Station Road in January 1965 was a torrid affair! It was only a few weeks since the French had caught Great Britain on the hop in Perpignan and the British boys were determined that lightning would not strike twice. The French were also set on repeating the result to secure one of their few victories in this country. The mixture of feelings could only lead to an explosive atmosphere on the field. Great Britain went for five changes from the side which lost in France. In came Ray Ashby at full back for Ken Gowers, Neil Fox in the centre for Dick Gemmell, Ken Roberts at field side prop for John Warlow, Brian Tyson at blind side prop for John Tembey and Doug Walton of Castleford came in at loose forward for Harry Poole. The full side was Ray Ashby [Wigan]; Berwyn Jones [Wakefield Trinity], Frank Myler [Widnes], Neil Fox [Wakefield

Trinity], Johnny Stopford [Swinton]; Alan Hardisty [Castleford], Alex Murphy [St Helens, captain]; Ken Roberts [Halifax], Bob Dagnall [St Helens], Brian Tyson [Hull Kingston Rovers], Geoff Gunney [Hunslet], Bill Holliday [Whitehaven] and Doug Walton [Castleford].

France selected a trusted 13 in Pierre Lacaze [Toulouse]; Guy Bruzy [Perpignan], Jean-Pierre Lecompte [St Gaudens], Bertrand Ballouhey [Villeneuve], Andre Doulieu [Marseille]; Etienne Courtine [Villeneuve], Roger Garnung [Bordeaux]; Jean Pano [Villeneuve], Rene Segura [Carcassonne], Marcel Bescos [Limoux captain], Georges Ailleres [Toulouse], Jean Poux [Lezignan] and Jean-Pierre Clar [Villeneuve]. The referee was the excellent Mr D.T.H. Davies of Manchester who, during this extremely thorny game, experienced what can only be described as a referee's nightmare! The French were well on top in the first 40 minutes and played some sparkling stuff, although these moments of brilliance were offset by several bouts of one-on-one skirmishes!

On 15 minutes the clever Bertrand Ballhouhey stepped neatly through the first line of the British defence to send the exciting Guy Bruzy gliding over for a super try. Pierre Lacaze converted this try, to add to the very early penalty goal he had kicked. Britain pulled themselves together with the help of two Neil Fox penalty goals to go in at half time with the score France 7 Great Britain 4.

During the second half, Neil Fox landed two beautiful penalty goals to give Great Britain the lead, 8–7. After 62 minutes of play, a scrum erupted in a free for all with all 12 forwards fighting it out. Mr Davies quietened things down and awarded Britain a penalty kick. The dreaded moment for the referee had arrived.

The French captain, the ultra bullish prop Marcel Bescos would not retreat the mandatory 10 yards and was obviously upset at the awarded penalty. This game was live on BBC *Grandstand* with millions watching! Mr Davies had no option but to send off Bescos who was still remonstrating with the referee. Surrounded by his team mates, Bescos continued complaining to such an extent that the police entered the proceedings, mainly to remove the excited French officials, journalists and photographers who had charged onto the field in support of Bescos!

The French touch judge, Monsieur Jameau finally managed to talk the French captain off the field of play and escorted him to the touchline but Bescos returned to the field after a few seconds. Mr Davies advised Bescos to leave the field again but he refused, so Mr Davies of Manchester simply walked off the field himself, accompanied by several Frenchmen! As the game was televised nationally, things were delicate to say the least. Five minutes later with Mr Davies back on the field, without a weeping Monsieur Bescos, play resumed. Only Mr Davies's experience saved the game from becoming a total French farce.

The volatile part of French nature that is sometimes used unfairly against them became evident as they appeared to lose their drive and fervour after Bescos's departure. The whole French team stopped after they lost the ball in a tackle. Brian Tyson hacked on for Berwyn Jones to, once again, use his speed and tap the ball over the French line to score. Neil Fox finished the game with seven goals and both teams scored one try each through Jones and Bruzy with Pierre Lacaze landing two goals for France.

It was a most unusual international match which brought bad tempers to the fore. The situation concerning Bescos was in itself unacceptable—especially as the incident occurred for all to see on TV. Until the Bescos saga, France gave a good account of themselves but with a man short and self confidence oozing out of them, the strength of the British team and goal kicking skills of Neil Fox took its toll on the volatile visitors. Frank had an excellent second half and formed a powerful partnership with the strapping Neil Fox in the centre. The pair were hard working in both attack and defence.

The 1964–65 season was not a highly successful one for Widnes in either cup or league. As well as a defeat by Swinton in the Lancashire Cup in round two, further disappointment was waiting in the Challenge Cup when a strong and belligerent Workington Town came to Naughton Park in round one and forced a draw, by 2 points apiece, in a real physical battle. The following Wednesday's replay was another titanic struggle in heavy, clinging mud. After 80 minutes of biff, bang, wallop, Workington were victorious by the closest of scores, 2–0! Two losses to St Helens and Warrington, home and away, were eased by a terrific double over Widnes's old foes, Wigan.

The first 10–3 victory at Central Park on 14 November was gained by an extraordinary display of defensive work by the whole of the Widnes side. Tries by Jim Measures and Bob Chisnall with goals by Derek Heyes and Frank Myler gave the heroic Widnes their 10 points and the brilliant defence restricted Wigan, with all their superb players on view, to one solitary try. The Widnes side that day was, Derek Heyes; Bobby Chisnall, Alan Briers, Arnold Mort, Johnny Gaydon; Frank Myler, Mal Farmer; Wally Hurstfield, Tony Karalius, Brian Larkin, Ken Parton, Jim Measures and Vince Karalius.

The second victory against Wigan was at Naughton Park on 12 April when Widnes were involved in the end of season fixture pile up and actually played five games in 14 days! Widnes produced an emphatic 18–0 win in this game. Because of the congestion of matches, an unusual Widnes side again blotted out what looked like a very good Wigan side on paper. Widnes fielded Robin Whitfield; Heyes, Alan Jones, Ged Lowe, Gaydon; Frank Myler, Ged Smith; Larkin, Tony Karalius, Alan Walsh, Brian Winstanley, Doug Davies and Arthur Hughes. Widnes registered tries from Jones, Whitfield, Gaydon and Davies with Whitfield landing three goals. Such an outstanding performance showed the wealth of reserve talent at the Widnes club. Another point about these two games was that Frank was at stand off, his favourite position, in both games.

Frank looked forward to the 1965–66 season as it was New Zealand's turn to tour England. It was also a crucial season for all British players as the Lions tour of Australia and New Zealand would begin at the season's end. Frank also realised that selection for Lancashire County against the touring Kiwis was a vital cog in the selection for the end of season tour down under. His priorities were there in front of him. He needed a good, consistent season for his club in order to represent his county again particularly against the touring Kiwis. This in turn would help him gain selection for Great Britain in the Kiwi Test series culminating in his selection for the 1966 tour of Australia and New Zealand.

Despite all Frank's good intentions, this particular season turned out to be one of Frank's worst for niggling injuries and he missed the first five games of the season. He returned in time to play in the centre against the touring Kiwis and score a Myler 'special' try in the game. Widnes hosted the match against New Zealand at Naughton Park on 6 September and once again Widnes produced a superb display of defensive rugby league restricting the tourists to only one try during the whole game. The Widnes team that day was Whitfield; Gaydon, Keith Northey, Frank Myler, Mal Aspey; Lowe, Smith; Larkin, George Kemel, Walsh, Measures, Winstanley and Vince Karalius, with Joe Argent as forward substitute. Widnes achieved their 8–3 victory over the Kiwis through great determination and a wonderful team spirit. Their two tries were scored by Frank and Keith Northey with Robin Whitfield kicking one goal.

On 20 September Lancashire county played Cumberland at Whitehaven and Frank was selected to play in the centre partnering Bill Burgess of Barrow on his wing. Willie Aspinall of Warrington was at stand off half and his half back partner was Frankie Parr of Wigan. Lancashire's team was Ken Gowers [Swinton]; Bill Burgess [Barrow], Frank Myler [Widnes], Jackie Melling [Warrington], Johnny Stopford [Swinton]; Willie Aspinall [Warrington], Frankie Parr [Wigan]; Danny Gardiner [Wigan], George Kemel [Widnes], Ken Roberts [Halifax], Terry Fogerty [Halifax], Roy Evans [Wigan] and Doug Laughton [St Helens]. Cumberland's selection had a strong look to it, with quick backs and a big tough pack! Their side was Paul Charlton [Workington Town]; Tony Colloby [Workington Town], Eric Bell [Workington Town], Les Bettinson [Salford], Ike Southward [Workington Town]; Phil Kitchen [Whitehaven], Bill Smith [Workington Town]; Brian Edgar [Workington Town], Tom Hill [Whitehaven], Les Moore [Whitehaven], Matt McLeod [Whitehaven], Bill Holliday [Hull Kingston Rovers] and Johnny Rae [Bradford Northern], with Harry Archer [Workington] as back substitute. The referee was Mr Laurie Gant of Wakefield and the attendance was 4,300.

Cumberland scored two tries to Lancashire's one with honours even in the goal kicking stakes, Ken Gowers and Bill Holliday landing four goals each for their teams. Cumberland's tries came from Johnny Rae and Harry Archer on as a substitute for Ike Southward. Lancashire's try came from Bill Burgess who finished off a smart break by Frank Myler.

September was a busy month for Frank as he was confirmed as one of the Great Britain centres selected to play in the first Test match against New Zealand at Station Road, Swinton on 25 September 1965. Britain went into this game with seven men on international debut. One of these newcomers was playing on the wing outside Frank, he was Geoff Wriglesworth of the Leeds club. The other six were Ken Senior (wingman), Phil Kitchen (stand off), Danny Gardiner (prop), George Kemel (hooker), Mervyn Hicks (second row) and Charlie Renilson (loose forward). Around 8,500 spectators watched a dull sort of a game, possibly due to the fact that Britain had too many inexperienced players on view. These men were all good players at club level and the policy of the British selectors had almost always been to blood new international players in no more than two at a time. On top of this, the Kiwis played rough and ready, no doubt intending to give the seven new men a shock baptism into Test football. The brutal Kiwi pack made the British six work very hard indeed before the home side could claim a 7–2 victory in one of the drabbest Test matches in memory.

Great Britain called on, Ken Gowers [Swinton]; Geoff Wriglesworth [Leeds], Frank Myler [Widnes], Geoff Shelton [Hunslet], Ken Senior [Huddersfield]; Phil Kitchen [Whitehaven], Tommy Smales [Bradford Northern]; Danny Gardiner [Wigan], George Kemel [Widnes], Ken Roberts [Halifax], Mervyn Hicks [St Helens], Bill Holliday [Hull Kingston Rovers] and Charlie Renilson [Halifax]. There was a wee bit of strife amongst one or two of the debutants, as they thought that a couple of senior players were keeping the ball away from them for some reason or another. For instance, Phil Kitchen swears to this day that he received only two passes from the base of the scrum during the entire game. This tactic completely nullified the pace and power of the two British centres, Frank and Geoff Shelton, although both managed to produce fair games under the circumstances. The Kiwi side, with their immensely strong front row of 'Maunga' Emery, Colin O'Neil and Sam Edwards maintained this forward struggle, and were determined to keep play secured in midfield. The only try of the game came from the continued ploy of Tommy Smales of hitting the blind side of the scrum. This time from a close in scrum, the half back again ran to the blind side and sent a reverse back pass to his supporting loose forward, Charlie Renilson who accepted the flick and walked over the whitewash for a well worked try. This win against New Zealand did not satisfy many of the rugby league management committee. They could afford to be very selective in those days, as there was a wealth of young talent coming through.

Frank had also received notification of selection for Lancashire County to play against the Kiwis on Wednesday 13 October at St Helens. But Widnes had an important tie in the Floodlit Cup on Tuesday 12 October. Frank's allegiance to the Widnes cause held true and he declared himself available to play against Warrington at Wilderspool on the evening before the county game against New Zealand. He scored another memorable try in the Chemic's 20–10 victory. The other try scorers at Warrington were Frank Collier, Tony Karalius and Johnny Gaydon with Robin Whitfield kicking four goals. The Widnes team on duty that evening were Whitfield; Aspey, Briers, Frank Myler, Gaydon; Lowe, Walker; Collier, Tony Karalius, Walsh, Larkin, Winstanley and Vince Karalius. The day after this great away win for the club, Frank was on his way across to Knowsley Road to join up with his Lancashire County team mates to play in yet another challenging game against international opposition.

The Kiwis competed very well against the full Great Britain side losing the first Test 7–2 and the second Test 15–9. The third Test ended in a 9 points all draw. In the county and club fixtures the Kiwis lost seven games against Yorkshire, Bradford Northern, Widnes, St Helens, Whitehaven, Swinton and Wakefield Trinity but were successful against Lancashire and the Commonwealth XIII side. They won the other 11 fixtures against club sides.

Lancashire wanted desperately to emulate the White Rose Counties win over the tourists. The side selected to wear the red and white of Lancashire was Ken Gowers [Swinton]; Bill Burgess [Barrow], Jackie Melling [Warrington], Alan Buckley [Swinton], Brian Glover [Warrington]; Frank Myler [Widnes], Tommy Bishop [Barrow]; Peter Birchall [Rochdale Hornets], George Kemel [Widnes], Ken Roberts [Halifax], Terry Fogerty [Halifax], Brian Simpson [Swinton] and Dave Robinson [Swinton]. The required result was not forthcoming in this game as the almost Test strength Kiwis proved to be a little too good on the day. The New Zealand team which won by 21–10 was Jack Fagan; Pat White, Robin Strong, Graham Kennedy, Roy Christian; Roger Bailey, Bob Irvine; 'Maunga' Emery, Bill Schultz, Robin Scholefield, Robin Orchard, Don Hammond and Graham Mattson. The attendance was 8,700 and the referee was Mr Harry Pickersgill of Halifax.

Frank enjoyed the tough competition against the Test utility back Roger Bailey who was quick, elusive and a hard defender at stand off half. For Lancashire, Frank, Alan Buckley, Dave Robinson and the Halifax pair, Terry Fogerty and Ken Roberts played well. Alan Buckley and Brian Simpson scored tries, with Ken Gowers landing two goals, making the county scorers an all Swinton affair. The Kiwis' 21 points were achieved by tries from Robin Orchard and Graham Mattson (2) with Jack Fagan goals (2) and Graham Kennedy goals (4) landing the two pointers.

Despite the win by Great Britain over New Zealand in the first Test, the international selectors made eight changes for the second Test at Odsal. In came Paul Charlton at full back for Ken Gowers. Bill Burgess and Johnny Stopford were on the wings for Geoff Wriglesworth and Ken Senior and Alan Buckley was in the centre for Frank Myler with Alan Hardisty at stand off for the unfortunate Phil Kitchen. Ken Roberts moved across from number 10 to number 8 in place of Danny Gardiner, Bill Ramsey came into the second row for Mervyn Hicks, and Johnny Rae was in at loose forward for Charlie Renilson. As there was a tour to Australia and New Zealand at the end of this season, changes were expected at international level as the selectors looked at as many candidates as possible. Frank realised that this was his biggest chance to tour. His age and experience were just right for a tour spot especially with his ability to play in top company both in the centre and at stand off. He had experience of playing against touring teams at inter-county level and the consistency of his play would be a bonus on tour. All he could do now was sit back, keep his form at Widnes and wait to see what would happen.

Frank's form was as consistently good as ever for Widnes and Lancashire County maintained their faith in him, selecting Frank in October 1965 after the disappointing Test match the previous month. Frank accepted that the selectors had to run the rule over as many combinations of players as possible before announcing the touring team and there were four more Tests against France and New Zealand before the tour team was selected. Unfortunately Frank was overlooked for all four Tests and the thought of missing this chance of a lifetime to tour was overpowering. The Widnes game at Huddersfield in mid October

1965 was the last game Frank played until his return from injury on 5 February in the game at Post Office Road against Featherstone Rovers.

Frank realised that his lengthy injury had come at a very bad time for him and he had to find his true form as soon as possible if he was to make the touring squad. On his fifth game back against Rochdale Hornets away, everything clicked into place and Frank blasted in for a great hat trick of tries. Playing almost totally in the centre, Frank's aspirations were realised when RLHQ contacted him, advised him that he would be in the touring squad and should make all arrangements to be away from home and family for three months. Dates were set for the official meeting of the touring team, being measured for blazers, trousers, etc, medicals, signing of the tour contracts and terms of payment—all the incidental things that take place pre tour. The RFL advised all the players that they should notify the RFL about any injury sustained for their club between now and the embarkation of the tour and they must send regular updates of any injury to RLHQ.

But all the tourists had a responsibility to their club too. In the run in to the end of the season, Widnes were still in the Challenge Cup having beaten the Yorkshire junior side Brookhouse from Wakefield. The draw for round two took Widnes into a hard tie at home to Bradford Northern. The Widnes side that played Northern on that day was Whitfield; Northey, Aspey, Frank Myler, Gaydon; Lowe, Boylan; Hurstfield, Kemel, Collier, Parton, Larkin and Vince Karalius.

Despite having a strong team out against them, Bradford Northern won 7–6 in a thriller. Frank didn't miss a match in the remaining league games after hearing of his tour selection. Wins against Liverpool City, Dewsbury twice, Whitehaven, Blackpool Borough and Barrow followed the Bradford Northern cup tie. Defeats came against Liverpool City 10–0 and Leigh 8–2, both away, before Widnes travelled to Central Park to face Wigan in the new styled top-16 play off for the Championship. Although Widnes tried hard, the chips were against them and they were beaten 27–10.

For Frank, it was all systems go for the tour as the day for the departure came nearer. This could be the trip of a lifetime.

10

PLAYING ON TOUR IN AUSTRALIA

The Great Britain Rugby League Lions squad to tour Australia and New Zealand in 1966 was a selected bunch of excellent players. Led by the experienced team managers Mr W. Spaven of Hull Kingston Rovers and Mr J. Errock of Oldham and skippered by Harry Poole of Leeds, the team had to allow for Alex Murphy of St Helens withdrawing from the squad having gained selection for the third consecutive tour. Speedy Ian Brooke of Bradford Northern took his place and he played in all five Test matches on the tour. The full touring squad was Arthur Keegan [Hull FC], Ken Gowers [Swinton], Bill Burgess [Barrow], Johnny Stopford [Swinton], Berwyn Jones [Wakefield Trinity], Geoff Wriglesworth [Leeds], Ian Brooke [Bradford Northern], Geoff Shelton [Hunslet], Frank Myler [Widnes], Alan Buckley [Swinton], Willie Aspinall [Warrington], Alan Hardisty [Castleford], Tommy Bishop [St Helens], Carl Dooler [Featherstone Rovers], Brian Edgar [Workington Town], Ken Roberts [Halifax], Cliff Watson [St Helens], Geoff Crewdson [Keighley], Colin Clarke [Wigan], Peter Flanagan [Hull Kingston Rovers], John Mantle [St Helens], Bill Ramsey [Hunslet], Bill Bryant [Castleford], Terry Fogerty [Halifax], Dave Robinson [Swinton] and Harry Poole [Leeds captain]. The physiotherapist was 'Paddy' Armour of Wakefield Trinity.

In 1988, Frank set down his memoirs as a record of the 1966 tour and of the two further tours he took part in, one as captain in 1970 and the other as coach in 1984. He recalls that great experience of 1966:

When I first set foot in Australia, I had been playing professional rugby league for 10 years. I had already represented my country in many international matches against New Zealand and France and played against the Australians both in club games against the Kangaroo tourists and in the winning Great Britain team in the 1960 World Cup competition. I thought I knew pretty much everything there was to know about the game. But I was wrong! Until you have been on tour your rugby education is incomplete.

The first lesson one learns is about travelling. On a rugby league tour your whole life is taken over by a pre-arranged timetable! On this 1966 tour we landed in Darwin one day. The very next day we were playing! There was no nonsense about jet lag or acclimatisation; you just had to get on with the job you were there for. We had some fun on the tour but the overriding memories are of playing, travelling, struggling to get over injuries, travelling, trying to prepare both mentally and physically for the next game and travelling! Unless one has been on tour in Australia it is impossible to imagine just how much time teams spend travelling. These days, as in my time there, the travelling is done almost totally by plane and this can be pretty bad if you are a poor plane traveller like me. My mother gave me a set of rosary beads before I left England with the touring team and I had them out more than once on some of those plane trips! I shared those rosary beads many times with my roommate and travelling companion, big Terry Fogerty and he wasn't even a Catholic! The beads were out and being used in one particular hairy trip from Queanbeyan to Sydney. Everything was fine until we ran into a dust storm and the pilot had to make an emergency landing in zero visibility at Wagga Wagga. I don't want an experience like that again!

What gets you through some sections of touring, such as being stranded for hours in a remote place or just the mind numbing monotony of hours of plane travel, is having a sense of humour. As in most team sports, there are plenty of natural born comedians around and in 1966 we had plenty who could turn the dreariest waiting hours into a riot of laughter. But not all the real characters on tour are the players. On the long tours we had back then we were travelling all over Australia and New Zealand and sometimes New Guinea, not only with the 26 players and staff but with a party of 35 to 40 people! The groups were made up of pressmen who had to send home regular details of games played and the general happenings on tour to their daily or Sunday newspapers. One of the best writers and a wonderful character, Phil King writer for the *Sunday People*, was a man I grew to know very well. Phil is now unfortunately no longer with us but he was a great guy. He was only five feet three inches in height and weighed in at 17 stones. Full of life, one of his passions was that he loved to gamble. He would bet on anything from greyhounds to pigeon racing and he loved to play cards with the lads!

Stranded one day up in Rockhampton in Queensland, waiting for four hours for a replacement plane as our original craft had broken down, it wasn't long before a gang of 10 or so, Phil included, pushed four coffee tables together and started playing 'Shoot', a favourite card game of the lads. Some of the others were in the bar and some went mooching around just having a look at things in general. Geoff Wriglesworth was one of these moochers and he found an enormous black toad with bulging red eyes. It really was a repulsive creature and hardly any of the lads would have dared to touch it let alone pick it up as Geoff did. It had claws that could grip rather than the usual kind of frog feet.

The Shoot game had reached a tense moment with a big kitty. Totally engrossed in the card game, Phil King failed to notice Geoff close to him and the York farm lad slipped the great black toad gently into his lap! The toad sat there for a few seconds before it moved a little and Phil looked down, straight into those huge red eyes. Phil's eyes bulged bigger than the toads but he was too paralysed with shock and fright to speak! Remaining in his chair, he simply fell backwards, away, he hoped, from this huge monster perched on his lap. Unfortunately, far from dislodging it the toad only gripped more tightly. I can still picture Phil, flat on his back, staring in horror at this monster toad which had now hopped onto his chest! The creature was staring menacingly with its ruby red eyes only inches away from Phil's face whilst everyone in the room was hysterical with laughter. This was too much for Phil who swept the toad away from him and regained his feet. Tears were running down everyone's face and the laughter was deafening—no one was laughing louder than me!

My reputation as a practical joker as well as the fact that I had been sat next to him playing cards and that I was now laughing almost out of control, convinced Phil that I was the culprit of the deed. Scarlet faced, Phil turned on me and snarled, 'Right Myler you b*****d, you've picked on the wrong man this time! You'll learn my lad. The pen is mightier than the sword'.

Everything went quiet as they realised that Phil was not well pleased but I couldn't stop myself answering, 'Yes Phil, but is it mightier than the toad?' which set the lads off laughing again. This was a bad move on my part as Phil was 100 per cent sure that I was the toad man and he was true to his word as I never had a good write up from him for the remainder of the tour. The fans back home reading the reports in the *Sunday People* in 1966 never realised that Phil's match coverage was biased by the memory of a huge black toad with big, red eyes, as Phil neglected to mention this incident!

Phil and his gambling exploits were involved once again in an evening of boxing we attended in Sydney. As I was entering the hall, one of the locals spotted my blazer badge and asked me if I was going to have a wager on any of the boxers that evening. I replied that because I didn't know any of the boxers I wouldn't be having a bet. The local responded, 'Well just in case you do fancy a flutter, remember they always put the champion in the red corner and the challenger in the blue corner. So don't back the blue corner unless they give you good odds.'

Sitting down to watch the fights I found that Phil was sitting next to me and he asked, 'Shall we have a friendly bet Frank?'

I replied, 'There's not much point when we don't know the fighters'.

Phil's gambling instincts meant that he couldn't bear to sit through the whole evening without a flutter on the result. 'Go on Frank, just for the interest. Two dollars a fight and I'll take the blue corner.' Well how could I refuse this?

Phil was 12 dollars down (give or take a couple of dollars) with one fight to go. His hopes were now pinned on the final blue corner boxer, a huge Maori with rippling muscles. Within a few seconds of this fight, the big Maori flattened my man and was doing a victory Haka around the ring when my fighter got back onto his feet, caught the big Maori off guard and biff, Phil lost again as his man was counted out!

The tour began with that first game the day after arriving in Darwin against Northern Territory which the tourists won by 17–7. The local boys played it tough without possessing the skilful finesse required to inflict a defeat on the Lions but the Brits knew they had arrived in Australia all right. Another point driven home early in the tour was that we all had to put up with practical jokes which were rife especially amongst those of us who had joked most of their life, such as me and the younger players. We had to keep these jokes under control so as not to hurt the butt of the joke or to insult or scare anyone not on the touring squad. The jokes helped to take our minds off the pressures that came with living, eating and sleeping with the sole idea of beating the Aussies in the Tests. Living together for just over three months meant we got to know each other's little fads, habits and weaknesses.

Take Terry Fogerty for instance. Have you ever seen anyone lay in bed to clean his shoes? Or has anyone ever thought how Peter Flanagan earned the nickname 'Flash' Flanagan? This star of both the 1966 and the 1970 tours was a typical cocky, bustling little hooker who stood around 5' 8'. He was a flashy dresser, smartly turned out with brightly coloured ties, shirts and socks! He was a nice young bloke who always had a smile on his face and was the life and soul of the tour. But Flash had one unusual weakness. He was, to put it kindly, rather wary about animals, birds and reptiles. It was strange that a hard as nails rugby league forward couldn't stand being near even the smallest, most harmless animal.

There are plenty of unusual creatures in Australia, and once the practical jokers found out about Flash's little weakness, we were on the lookout for jokes to play on him.

Darwin was the place we tried our first trick on him. It is sub tropical up there and because of the heat generated, day and night, the humidity makes it impossible to sleep under covers. So Flash stripped off and slept in the 'noddy'. On the plane approaching Darwin, the lads told Flash that Darwin had the most species of snakes in the world with deadly venom. In the hotel we laid our plans very carefully. We knew Flash would go to bed early and one of our jokers slipped out to retrieve the perfectly harmless, beautifully coloured grass snake we had caught earlier. He nipped up to Flash's room and laid the docile reptile under the thin cotton sheet that Flash used to cover his feet with. The snake was about 3 feet long with a flickering tongue which darted out regularly.

As I said earlier, the snake was perfectly harmless and quite happy under the sheet on Flash's bed. We all waited outside Flash's room on the veranda with cameras at the ready. We didn't have to wait long. The warm peaceful night was disturbed by a low moan of disbelief. We peeped through the Venetian blinds to see how Flash would react to finding a snake as his bedfellow. We saw Flash, naked, one leg in bed and the other out on the floor of the bedroom. Then, with loud yell of horror, without waiting to grab any clothes, he fled at great speed into the corridor. We were in hysterics and had lots of pictures of Flash's backside disappearing out of the room. We were certain about one thing: Flash didn't like snakes at all!

We were invited to a Nature Reserve whilst in Brisbane. There were all kinds of strange animals scampering around and what seemed like thousands of brightly coloured squawking birds above us. From time to time, a brilliantly coloured bird swooped down from the sky and squawked suddenly just above our heads. This was not Flash's cup of tea at all. He walked about in a crouched position, ducking like a boxer every time he heard a squawk. 'What the hell are these things Frank?' he asked me, still ducking and weaving away from the squawks.

Keeping a straight face, I answered, 'They're some kind of budgie Flash. They say they never attack humans unless they sense that someone is really frightened of them'.

Flash took a quick look up into the sky and made a dash for a big group of visitors. He pushed into the middle of the group deciding there was safety in numbers. Regaining his composure later, Flash rejoined our little group and we wandered over to where the remainder of our players were stood in a circle, obviously watching something of interest. Flash was full of himself again and he pushed his way to the front to see what was going on. He was just in time to witness Brian Edgar having his photo taken with a giant python around his neck. The snake must have been 12 feet long and about a foot thick. As soon as Flash reached the front, the snake looked straight at Flash standing only feet away from him, opened its big mouth and hissed. This was too much for Flash who ran like hell for the safety of the bus!

The attendance in Darwin was expected to be sparse. In 1966, the area was not populated to the extent it is today. A crowd of 2,965 saw the game. As the tourists' next game was against Far North Queensland, played in the beautiful tropical area of Cairns, it involved an air trip of around 1,700km. This was the type of travelling mentioned in Frank's memoirs as the team descended down the North Eastern seaboard of Australia on their way to the first Test venue of the Sydney Cricket Ground.

The tourists won the game at Cairns against Far North Queensland 48–7 on a bone hard ground. Again the attendance was above average for the club games in the area, a crowd of 4,577 saw the game but already there were sore feet in the tourist's camp as even the shortest of studs began to rub skin off the extreme edges of toes, heels and soles.

A 300km trip down the coast to Townsville was next and a shock awaited the tourists as a strong North Queensland outfit beat them 17–15 before a sell out crowd of 6,000. The result was aided by some dreadful calls by the referee who seemed to be against the Brits. The squad flew a further 600km down the coast to line up against Central Queensland and another 10–5 loss. Unfortunately the game at Rockhampton drew in only 2,860 spectators. From there they flew 1,200km to New South Wales to take on a side whose players were all determined to make the first Test team in a few weeks' time. That team was Sydney, a side composed of players in the Sydney league, from the likes of Balmain, Western Suburbs, Parramatta, Newtown and St George. The game was played on the Sydney Cricket Ground before an attendance of 38,831. In a real brawl of a game, the Lions tourists emerged winners by 15–14 in a ding-dong encounter which was about par for a big game in Sydney. The Aussies loved to watch the Great Britain style of play where big forwards could side step and handle the ball like backs!

Next the touring team travelled to Wollongong a mere 50km down the coast from Sydney. Their opponents were another solid outfit, Southern New South Wales. This was always a testing game for touring sides and was nearly always slipped in as the match before the first Test match. Playing with real zest, the Aussie boys produced a fine performance to register a 17–8 victory over the tourists.

Looking back through the history of tours it was considered common practice to take 26 players, two for every position. This was because the teams played so many games in such a comparatively short period that the team needed cover in case of injury. The Test team, in those early days, was prepared and the 13 not playing in the big games would bear the brunt of playing games, very quickly, one after the other. The men not selected for Test matches were known as 'ham'n' eggers'.

Frank's memoirs continued:

We had our fair share of injuries on this tour. The old system of selecting a team to give the Test players a rest in the 'country' games went out of the window as very often the teams for these games picked themselves. The question asked of the whole squad was, 'Who is fit enough to play?' so there was no danger of the ham'n' eggers label being attached to anyone. Whoever arranged the playing itinerary for this tour must have been either a sadist or simply crackers! The highest number of games ever played on the Australian leg of the tour up to our tour was 22 by the 1954 squad. We played 23 games with an injury depleted squad! Of course no replacements were flown out in those days. If half the squad were out injured you had to soldier on with what you had left. I had some unusual injuries on the tour, such as breaking my hand in an up country game by handing off a tackle. I scored a try doing it but I would have rather have missed that try as it ruled me out of the first Test.

An even more unexpected problem came with my feet. During 1966 Australia was in the middle of a drought. Severe bush fires raged and farmers were in real danger of losing all their stock. The football fields all over Australia were like rock. After playing a few games on this tour my feet were in a bad way. Constant pounding on the iron hard ground made my boots so uncomfortable that it was sheer agony to put them on. Things became so bad that in one game I had to stop playing and examine my feet. The bottom blisters had burst and new ones formed on top of them. I literally had blisters on blisters! It was impossible for me to put my boots back on so I ran back into the field of play in my socks. When the referee spotted what I had done he sent me off for being improperly dressed for play! The problems with my feet were so serious that I thought I would not be able to play again on the tour. In the end I was saved by a tip from the Aussie forward Noel 'Ned' Kelly from Queensland. He told me to smear the inside of both socks with Vaseline and do the same on the outside of the socks. Finally I had to smear the insides of both boots. All this Vaseline gave my feet insulation from the friction that was causing the blisters. With the help of this tip I was able to get through the rest of the tour. Thank you Noel!

By far the worst blow to the whole tour, though, was the injury to the captain, Harry Poole. Harry had unluckily picked up a groin tear the week before the first Test. I was unavailable because of my broken hand and I was sick about that. But I felt sicker for Harry. He had a great tour up until then and he was not just a great captain, he was a great player as well. The injury was so severe that he never played in a single Test match on the Australian leg of the tour.

The Great Britain side went into this Test match as massive underdogs, with stand-in captain Brian Edgar of Workington Town taking over from the injured Harry Poole. Their playing record to date was played 9 won 5 lost 4. The Great Britain team for the crucial game was Arthur Keegan [Hull FC]; Bill Burgess [Barrow], Ian Brooke [Bradford Northern], Alan Buckley [Swinton], Johnny Stopford [Swinton]; Alan Hardisty [Castleford], Tommy Bishop [St Helens]; Brian Edgar [Workington Town, captain], Peter Flanagan [Hull Kingston Rovers], Cliff Watson [St Helens], John Mantle [St Helens], Bill Bryant [Castleford] and Dave Robinson [Swinton]. The Australians were at strength with Keith Barnes [Balmain]; Ken Irvine [North Sydney], John McDonald [Toowoomba], Graeme Landlands [St George], Johnny King [St George]; Gary Banks [South Newcastle], Billy Smith [St George]; Ron Crowe [West Wyalong], Ian Walsh [St George captain], Lloyd Weier [North Sydney], Angelo Crema [Tully], Bill Bradstreet [Manly] and Johnny Raper [St George]. The referee was Mr J. Bradley of New South Wales, and the attendance was 57,962.

Led magnificently by Brian Edgar, Great Britain gained a lead after Keith Barnes had kicked a penalty goal. Then Cliff Watson blasted his way over from 20 yards, and Arthur Keegan landed a fine conversion. Two further Barnes penalties put the Aussies ahead by 6–5, but Keegan regained the advantage with a 40 yard accurate penalty goal.

After Tommy Bishop had added to the Brits' lead with a well taken drop goal, Alan Hardisty showed his class with a break from acting half back, a kick ahead and he found enough pace to beat Barnes in a straight race to dive on the ball for a magnificent try which Arthur Keegan converted. The Test was won when Bill Burgess was given a chance by Ian Brooke and he took it brilliantly by gliding around Johnny King and diving in at the corner flag. This gave the Brits a lead of 17–8 with six minutes to play. In the dying seconds Gary Banks chased a Barnes kick and claimed a try which Barnes converted. It was a wonderful victory for

the Lions despite the upset of losing their captain before the game.
Frank recalls:

Brian Edgar's experience on two previous tours in 1958 and 1962
stood him in good stead and he had an absolute blinder of a game.
The Aussies weren't used to a big forward who could side step on
a sixpence, stand in the tackle and pass around the back of the
tackler to his support players. He was brilliant. Alan Hardisty, on
his first tour, showed the Aussies a bit of his magic, and Tommy
Bishop had them wondering what he was made of as he blasted out
of tackle after tackle on those short bursts from the scrum base
and the play the ball. Tommy must have been one of the strongest
half backs ever to play the game. Even though I was only watching
the game, I felt just as pleased as if I had been out there playing.

Despite all the injuries, we had built up a strong Test team. We
had the invaluable experience of Brian Edgar and our young
players, particularly Hardisty and Bishop, had come good. The
Aussies, tormented by the genius and speed of Alex Murphy on
the two previous tours, breathed a sigh of relief when they
discovered that he was not making this trip. Instead they now had
to fathom a completely different type of scrum half. Every tour
throws up its discoveries and ours was Ian Brooke the centre from
Bradford Northern. Ian had probably just scraped into this tour as
fourth choice centre. By the end of the tour he had proved himself
to be the best! Ian was the ideal player for Australia, fearless, fast
and strong. He complemented perfectly the more subtle skills of
Alan Hardisty. Both these players played in all three Australian
Test matches.

We also had a strong pack of forwards with a fine blend of
physical power and deft ball handling. Both Brian Edgar and Cliff
Watson were great props on this tour. Above all we built up a great
team spirit both on and off the field and this was the best
protection of all against the Aussie press which, of course, had a go
at us.

I find it difficult not to repeat the word 'we' constantly when talking about the tour. I use the 'we' so often because that is the way it has to be in Australia. If your squad doesn't function as a single unit you can get into a lot of trouble. This last factor is vitally important. After all, 28 people (including the team manager and coach) have to live in close proximity with each other for three months. It is quite easy to become fed up of seeing the same faces day after day. What you all have is a common purpose and a common enemy! It is a bit like being in the army. The purpose is to win every game against the common enemy. The lads playing in the up country games have their part to play, as our up country teams had a good smattering of regular Test players. We were all in it together. But it was crucial to win those Test matches.

I think the system we had for training on tour in those days helped. There was no coach on the tour. The tactical side of training, planned moves and combinations involving groups of players was in the hands of the captain and senior players. Nobody dictated. If a younger player wanted to try out a new idea then he took over and if we thought something would work after trying it out in training, we incorporated it into our game plan. This may seem a little haphazard or amateurish, but it is what modern day coaches use as a change from the boring day after day training programmes. Ideas coming from players often work better than those coaches impose on them. Stifling creativity is a sure way of producing boring, stereotype rugby that neither players nor fans enjoy. So we worked with each other and this helped to foster a closer spirit within the whole squad.

The feeling of comradeship we had in the three tours was not just down to team spirit, although it is a term I have used previously. Club teams can develop good team spirit on the field but when players end the game, change and go home they go away as individuals, or in pairs or small groups. On tour there is a completely different attitude and atmosphere. More to the point, there were no cliques and we were all conscious of our responsibilities to each other. This is remarkable when one realises that there were little groups of players from the same club or the same town and most of us had only met the others in league games or cup ties when we were trying to knock the hell out of each other.

We had no trouble on tour, there was no Lancashire–Yorkshire divide with us. It would have been awkward anyway as our new captain was a straight talking Cumbrian! We didn't do everything together of course. Only a few were mad enough to get up at four o'clock in the morning to get a round of golf in before the sun got too hot—like I did up in Darwin. There were no bad arguments, no 'bother', no fights. That was something special when you think of some of the rum characters, the amount of leg-pulling that went on, the practical jokes, not to mention the strain that we were under during the three months we were living together.

It would be wrong to call the non Test results in Australia a raging success. Going into the first Test, Great Britain lost the two games prior to the Test match as well as the two games immediately after the first Test. The second Test was in Brisbane so the squad travelled north again to play the Northern Division at Tamworth, inland from the coast on the edge of the Liverpool Plain. A big, rough team played hard throughout the game, the Northern Division always gave touring sides a rough ride but this time they excelled themselves with a grand 15–13 win over the tourists. They moved further north for the next game to take on a strong Brisbane side. Again the tourists were beaten 19–17. No doubt the strange decisions by rather partisan referees had much to do with the defeats.

The tourists were now in the Central Queensland leg of the tour and wins came against Queensland in Brisbane 38–29 before an attendance of over 23,000, Wide Bay at Bundaberg 30–22 and Ipswich on their own ground 44–10. In the game before the second Test, the team went inland to Toowoomba to take on the tough locals. Then it was back across to Brisbane for the crucial second Test. Frank had proved his fitness in a couple of the Queensland country games after his broken hand. The interest in this Test match was positive. The Aussies were one game to nil down. If they lost this then the ashes, recaptured so convincingly in

Britain in 1963, would be lost again to the Brits. The teams played before a sell out crowd of 45,057. Great Britain's team was Arthur Keegan [Hull FC]; Bill Burgess [Barrow], Ian Brooke [Bradford Northern], Frank Myler [Widnes], Geoff Wriglesworth [Leeds]; Alan Hardisty [Castleford], Tommy Bishop [St Helens]; Brian Edgar [Workington Town, captain], Peter Flanagan [Hull Kingston Rovers], Cliff Watson [St Helens], John Mantle [St Helens], Bill Ramsey [Hunslet] and Dave Robinson [Swinton].

Australia made seven changes—in the centre, at stand off, the two props and the whole back three—so intent were they to win this vital Test. The side was Keith Barnes [Balmain]; Ken Irvine [North Sydney], Graeme Langlands [St George], Johnny Greaves [Canterbury Bankstown], Johnny King [St George]; John Gleeson [Brisbane Brothers], Billy Smith [St George]; Noel Kelly [Western Suburbs], Ian Walsh [St George, captain], John Wittenberg [Theodore], Mick Veivers [Manly-Warringah], Dick Thornett [Parramatta] and Ron Lynch [Parramatta]. The referee was Mr Col Pearce of New South Wales.

This was only the third Test match in rugby league history that finished try-less. As described in Robert Gate's *Rugby League Lions: 100 Years of Test Matches* this was a vicious and bad tempered Test match and resulted in a victory Australia did not deserve. Great Britain played for the final 35 minutes with a man short. The fighting on the field spread onto the terraces as brawling broke out amongst the spectators and pockets of fighting spilled over onto the field. It was not a good day for the image of Australian sport. Wittenberg, the big Aussie prop, was the first to be laid out and from the ensuing penalty kick, Keith Barnes put Australia ahead after 8 minutes of play. The half time score was 2–0, as there was more fighting than football! Ian Brooke was felled by a stiff-arm tackle as he fielded the kick off and this seemed to be a declaration of war as the fists and feet went in at almost every tackle. Bill Ramsey was levelled in the first half and he gained revenge on 44 minutes but was despatched by referee Pearce for his trouble. Arthur Keegan made the score 2 points all. Soon after he gave Britain the lead with a second penalty goal. Barnes squared matters again at 4 points all with his second penalty goal. On the 68th minute, Britain could easily have put the match to bed as Geoff Wriglesworth raced in from his wing into the centres to make the extra man. Under pressure from a heavy tackle, the Leeds wingman was unable to feed Bill Burgess with an acceptable pass and the ball went to ground. On 76 minutes Barnes was awarded a simple penalty kick at goal and he landed the academic shot to give the Aussies a hard earned and rather fortunate victory.

There was only one game sandwiched in between the second and third Tests at Parkes, 300km across the Blue Mountains against Western Division. A capacity crowd of 8,000 packed into the neat little ground to watch Great Britain beat the local boys 38–11.

The final Test against the Aussies was, as usual, played at the Sydney Cricket Ground. Arthur Keegan and Frank Myler were left out and Ken Gowers and Alan Buckley took their places. Bill Bryant was the forward substitute and replaced John Mantle in the second half. The Aussies fielded three changes from the middle Test team, Peter Dimond the big, tough centre came in for Graeme Langlands and the great Arthur Beetson replaced Dick Thornett in the second row. Thornett came on in the second half as a substitute for Beetson. The other change was at full back where Les Johns took over from Keith Barnes. Robert Gate again supplies the details and describes the game as an all ticket sell out, action packed, incident laden thriller!

This game, of course, would determine the home of the Ashes Cup for another year as the series hung on a one all result with this being the decider. Col Pearce again was the referee and the gate was a massive 63,503! The teams were Australia, Les Johns [Canterbury Bankstown]; Ken Irvine [North Sydney], Peter Dimond [Western Suburbs], Johnny Greaves [Canterbury Bankstown], Johnny King [St George]; John Gleeson [Brisbane Brothers], Billy Smith [St George]; Noel Kelly [Western Suburbs], Ian Walsh [St George, captain], John Wittenberg [Theodore], Mick Veivers [Manly], Arthur Beetson [Balmain] and Ron Lynch [Parramatta]. Dick Thornett [Parramatta] was the forward substitute. Great Britain lined up, Ken Gowers [Swinton]; Bill Burgess [Barrow], Ian Brooke [Bradford Northern], Alan Buckley [Swinton], Geoff Wriglesworth [Leeds]; Alan Hardisty [Castleford], Tommy Bishop [St Helens]; Brian Edgar [Workington Town, captain], Peter Flanagan

[Hull Kingston Rovers], Cliff Watson [St Helens], John Mantle [St Helens], Bill Ramsey [Hunslet] and Dave Robinson [Swinton]. Bill Bryant [Castleford] was the forward substitute.

Although Australia scored five tries to two, they could not be sure of their Ashes success until the final whistle. The first of Ken Irvine's hat trick of tries came from a long, slightly forward pass from Beetson, the second was awarded following a blatant knock on by the wingman but allowed to play on and the third came from a dummying Les Johns run. Ron Lynch scored a fine individual try after a 30 yard break and Beetson made a try for Johnny King with a perfect kick through. Johns also added two goals. For the Brits, Alan Hardisty crossed twice, once for an interception try and long run and the other was a penalty try after Hardisty was obstructed, racing after a kick through. Ken Gowers landed four goals, but the Ashes stayed in Australia with this 19–14 win for the home nation. The bad feelings were seen at the very end of the game as Dave Robinson was knocked out from a vicious punch and this started an all out furious brawl involving all the players on the field and from the bench. The bell sounded to end the game as the fighting continued.

Only three games remained in Australia after the disappointment of losing the Ashes. Being on tour had been a real eye opener and a great experience for Frank. The first of the final three games in Australia meant travelling further into the bush than they had before. Around 450km south west of Sydney is Narrandera in the beautiful, rich Riverina district. The now weary tourists beat Riverina 34–20 and the squad moved back to Sydney to play their final game in that city against strong club side, Balmain. Almost 23,000 folk turned out to say farewell to this very likeable bunch of British players. Balmain won a fierce encounter 9–8 but the Brits left the field with their heads held high.

It was on to the last game of the 1966 tour in Australia. This was at Cooma in the deep south of New South Wales, a picturesque area between the Snowy Mountains and the Great Dividing Range, about 100km below Canberra. The game was against the Monaro District and the tourists signed off with a 33–12 win.

From there the tourists went across the Tasman Sea to face the Kiwis on their own soil. The first game on the Island of the Long White Cloud was at Huntly in the North Island, against Waikato. Their team had quite a few Maori players who all seemed to be big, strong athletes, who tackled very hard and very high! But the tourists' class told and they won 47–8. The second game was the first Test match against New Zealand played at Carlaw Park, Auckland. Frank found himself back in favour with the job of substitute back. The teams were, Great Britain, Ken Gowers [Swinton]; Bill Burgess [Barrow], Ian Brooke [Bradford Northern], Alan Buckley [Swinton], Geoff Wriglesworth [Leeds]; Alan Hardisty [Castleford], Tommy Bishop [St Helens]; Ken Roberts [Halifax], Colin Clarke [Wigan], Cliff Watson [St Helens], Harry Poole [Leeds captain], Bill Ramsey [Hunslet] and Dave Robinson [Swinton]. Frank took the place of Alan Hardisty, later in the game.

The Kiwis fielded a strong side for this first Test. Roger Tait [Auckland]; Brian Reidy [Auckland], Roy Christian [Auckland], Roger Bailey [Auckland], Bob Mincham [Auckland]; Graham Kennedy [West Coast], Graeme Farrar [Waikato captain]; Maunga Emery [Auckland], Col O'Neil [Wellington], Sam Edwards [Auckland], Eddie Moore [Auckland], Bill Deacon [Waikato] and Kevin Dixon [West Coast]. The referee was Mr John Percival of Auckland, and the gate was almost 15,000.

After the ultra tough ending to the Aussie part of the tour, this New Zealand series was like a walk in the park. For this first Test the Carlaw Park pitch was ankle deep in mud! The game was hard but fair. The style of play around the play the ball was typically strong Kiwi stuff with the two big, hard Maori props, 'Maunga' Emery and Sam Edwards being particularly powerful. These two men, along with hooker Col O'Neil, won an 11–6 scrum count during the game and Mr Percival awarded 18 penalties in favour of the Kiwis, yet Great Britain still continued in excellent form.

An Ian Brooke try and Ken Gower goal gave Britain the lead but Kiwi centre Roy Christian pulled back three points when he finished off a brilliant run by stand off Graham Kennedy. On the stroke of half time, Colin Clarke dived over for Ken Gower to convert to give Britain a 10–3 lead at the break. Frank Myler was almost over twice, with two fine efforts as he took over at stand off for the injured Alan Hardisty. But there was no stopping Frank Myler seconds later when he side stepped and dummied his way through a tight Kiwi defence to score a masterful try. Bill Burgess crossed after another fine break by Frank Myler and Ken Gowers landed two penalty goals and a superb drop goal from almost the half way line.

New Zealand struck when Sam Edwards slipped a great pass to Roy Christian who, in turn, released the very quick Bob Mincham and he sped half the length of the field to register a fine try, Graham Kennedy converting. Cliff Watson added a fifth try for the Lions when Tommy Bishop kicked through and Ian Brooke hacked on. Eddie Moore fumbled the ball in his own in goal area and Ian Brooke swooped onto the mistake only to lose the ball backwards himself. Up strolled Cliff Watson and simply touched the ball down to claim the try, Ken Gowers landing his fourth conversion to go with his great drop goal. So Great Britain won this first match 25–8 in New Zealand.

Next the team travelled down the North Island to play Wellington in the nation's capital city. Rugby league attendances were sparse in these rugby union strongholds and at the Wellington v Great Britain game, the crowd was a meagre 1,142. The tourists won 28–9 and crossed the Cook Straight to visit the long South Island of New Zealand. The attendance was slightly better at the match at Greymouth against West Coast, where 2,212 turned out in the rain to watch the tourists beat the locals 27–5. The last game in the South Island was in Christchurch against the Canterbury District team. The British played the game in exhibition style winning 53–6 at half pace before 1,192 hardy souls. The venue for the third from last game of the tour was the west coast of the North Island in the farming Taranaki district outside Auckland. Only 529 spectators saw the tourists beat Taranaki heavily 51–17 before the Great Britain squad moved for the final time up to Auckland.

The second Test and the final game of the tour against the tough Auckland district were the fixtures left to play. The Test match proved to be no contest as the Kiwis seemed to play with no determination. With their advantage of a 24 to 8 penalty count and a 10–4 scrimmaging win, it was difficult to imagine why the New Zealand offensive was ineffective. As it was Great Britain won 22–14, a score which is a poor reflection of the British team's superiority. The teams facing each other that 6 August were New Zealand, Brian Reidy [Auckland]; Ted Baker [Waikato], Roger

Bailey [Auckland], Roy Christian [Auckland], Willie Southorn [Taranaki]; Graham Kennedy [West Coast], Graeme Farrar [Waikato captain]; Sam Edwards [Auckland], Col O'Neil [Wellington], Robin Orchard [Bay of Plenty], Bill Deacon [Waikato], Garry Smith [Wellington] and Ernie Wiggs [Auckland].

Great Britain went with Ken Gowers [Swinton]; Bill Burgess [Barrow], Ian Brooke [Bradford Northern], Frank Myler [Widnes], Geoff Wriglesworth [Leeds]; Willie Aspinall [Warrington], Tommy Bishop [St Helens]; Ken Roberts [Halifax], Peter Flanagan [Hull Kingston Rovers], Cliff Watson [St Helens], Harry Poole [Leeds captain], Bill Ramsey [Hunslet] and Dave Robinson [Swinton]. Terry Fogerty [Halifax] was substitute forward and played in the second half. Mr Percival was again the referee and the gate at Carlaw Park was another poor 10,657. Try scorers for Great Britain were: Ian Brooke two tries, the first from a Frank Myler break, following a scrum win, his second from a cross field passing move, Bill Burgess raced in from Frank Myler's pass, and Willie Aspinall scored after Tommy Bishop had made the running, Ken Gowers landed five goals. Ernie Wiggs kicked seven excellent goals for the Kiwis.

The final game of the 1966 tour was against an Auckland side, almost Test strength, again at Carlaw Park. The British were determined to make a clean sweep of the New Zealand leg of the tour with a played 8, won 8 record. It was down to their fierce determination that they maintained their record with an unbelievably hard fought win against an Auckland team fired up to the brim! The score of Great Britain 12 Auckland 11 tells its own story. The tourists team for that final game were Keegan; Jones, Myler, Buckley, Wriglesworth; Aspinall, Dooler; Edgar, Flanagan, Watson, Clarke, Fogerty and Robinson. The forward substitute was Ken Roberts. The next day the squad was due to fly home after their three months' adventure and despite a touch of sadness that the trip was over, the players wanted to get home to their wives and children and pick up their lives again. Both the memories and friendships would last forever. The tour was something not to miss if given the chance.

11

FROM THE PALM TREES OF CAIRNS TO WIDNES

The 1966–67 season at Widnes began without Frank. The reason was that as Widnes kicked off on 13 August against Liverpool City away, Frank was engaged in a game in Christchurch, New Zealand. He was back on 2 September for the Lancashire Cup game at Naughton Park in the 26–13 win over Barrow. He was also back in the representative spotlight in a famous inter-county game at Headingley between Yorkshire and Lancashire. This was the first game ever played under the Leeds club's brand new floodlights which cost a staggering £15,000!

The game itself lived up to this historic setting with Frank having an outstanding game in the centre. The author was at the game and remembers vividly the defining moments of this terrific encounter. No fewer than 12 of the 1966 tourists were on view, five for Lancashire and seven for Yorkshire. The Yorkshire team lined up as Arthur Keegan [Hull FC]; Peter Godchild [Doncaster], Ian Brooke [Bradford Northern], Neil Fox [Wakefield Trinity], Geoff Wriglesworth [Leeds]; Mick Shoebottom [Leeds], Carl Dooler [Featherstone Rovers]; Dennis Hartley [Castleford], Peter Flanagan [Hull Kingston Rovers], Jack Scroby [Halifax], Terry Ramshaw [Halifax], Terry Clawson [Bradford Northern] and Harry Poole [Leeds]. Bill Bryant [Castleford] was the forward substitute and played in the second half. The Lancashire team was Colin Tyrer [Leigh]; Bill Burgess [Barrow], Frank Myler [Widnes], Billy Benyon [St Helens], Brian Glover [Warrington]; Willie Aspinall [Warrington], Tommy Bishop [St Helens]; Albert Halsall [St Helens], George Kemel [Widnes], Ivor Kelland [Barrow], Ray French

[St Helens], Fred Tomlinson [Barrow] and Dave Robinson [Swinton]. The referee was Mr H. Ostle of Aspatria and the attendance was 10,528.

The former Leeds RLFC team manager and schoolmaster of famous rugby league stronghold Kirkstall Road school, Ken Dalby, writes eloquently about this game in *The Headingley Story, Volume 4*, 'As the new floodlights were turned on, four clusters of stars gleamed out of a velvet sky but none shone more brightly than the Widnes centre Frank Myler'. That shows what an education can do for you! But Frank certainly educated the Yorkshire middle backs that evening with a five star performance against some good opponents. Tommy Bishop scored the first try off a sparkling side stepping opening from Frank. Then Peter Flanagan, Terry Clawson and Harry Poole combined to open the Lancashire defensive door and send Terry Ramshaw crashing over. Carl Dooler then prised open a gap for Neil Fox to power in and with big Neil landing two goals, as did Colin Tyrer, it was 10–7 to the White Rose at half time.

The highly competitive second half opened in explosive style as Ramshaw tore over for his second try of the game and Fox converted. Yorkshire had the look of winners but Ken Dalby again reflected, 'But Myler would have none of that. A thrust, a dummy, then a telling pass had Aspinall shimmering over for a classic try. A superb Tyrer conversion followed and the applause had hardly died down before the irrepressible Myler was gliding through again to create a super try for Glover. Still Myler called the tune and had Yorkshire back peddling with a neat kick through for Bishop just beaten by the bounce of the ball over the try line'. Glover used his strength to score the final try, converted by Tyrer to give Lancashire a 22–17 win.

Back at Widnes, Frank was playing mostly in the centre with the occasional game at stand off, in fact the ratio was 22 games wearing number 4 and six wearing number 6. A shock defeat in the Lancashire Cup away to Blackpool Borough by 19–7 was soon forgiven as the club began a seven game run without defeat. This run included a 17 points all draw with Hull FC at Naughton Park. At the beginning of December the two sides met again in the league at The Boulevard.

This game also ended in a 10 points all draw. Workington Town were beaten 15–8 at Naughton Park on 7 October and on 14 October, Swinton were beaten 18–3 at Station Road.

On Thursday 12 October, the same week Widnes beat Swinton, Frank was called into duty for the Lancashire v Cumberland inter-county game at Wilderspool, Warrington. The Lancashire team had a confident look about it as they had, after all, recently won a thriller under the new Leeds floodlights against Yorkshire. The side was Ken Gowers [Swinton]; Bill Burgess [Barrow], Frank Myler [Widnes], Billy Benyon [St Helens], Brian Glover [Warrington]; Willie Aspinall [Warrington], Graham Williams [Swinton]; Albert Halsall [St Helens], George Kemel [Widnes], Ivor Kelland [Barrow], Ray French [St Helens], Fred Tomlinson [Barrow] and Dave Robinson [Swinton].

Cumberland were playing for the county championship having drawn with Yorkshire at home. The team selected was Paul Charlton [Workington Town]; Bob Wear [Barrow], Les Bettinson [Salford], Eric Bell [Workington Town], Tony Colloby [Workington Town]; Harry Archer [Workington Town], Jack Newall [Workington Town]; Bill Martin [Workington Town], Mal Moss [Workington Town], Brian Edgar [Workington Town], Matt McLeod [Whitehaven], Dennis Martin [Workington Town] and Bill Pattinson [Workington Town]. The referee was Mr Peter Geraghty of York and the attendance was 5,716.

In a ding-dong struggle the result went the way of Cumberland as they scored four tries through Bob Wear, Les Bettinson and Bill Pattinson (2) to Lancashire's two tries from Dave Robinson. Paul Charlton kicked three goals for Cumberland and Ken Gower kicked four goals for Lancashire giving a final score of Cumberland 18 Lancashire 14. It was a spirited performance by the victors whose pack played in true Cumberland tradition.

In January 1967, Widnes suffered a heavy 46–2 defeat at Central park, Wigan. This was a shock to the club's system. January was also the month that Frank received the call to represent Great Britain again, this time against France at the Stade Albert Domec in Carcassonne. Only six of the recent tourists were selected for this international match. The team selected was Arthur Keegan [Hull FC]; Ian Hare

[Widnes], Frank Myler [Widnes], Neil Fox [Wakefield Trinity], Clive Sullivan [Hull FC]; Alan Hardisty [Castleford, captain], Keith Hepworth [Castleford]; Mick Harrison [Hull FC], Colin Clarke [Wigan], Brian Tyson [Hull Kingston Rovers], Terry Fogerty [Wigan], Bob Irving [Oldham] and Dave Robinson [Swinton]. Great Britain's substitutes were Roger Millward [Hull Kingston Rovers] and Bill Holliday [Hull Kingston Rovers].

France, looking for a win to give them six consecutive Test wins fielded Pierre Lacaze [Marseille]; Andre Ferren [Avignon], Guy Andrieu [Limoux], Claude Mantoulan [Perpignan], Jean-Claude Marty [Lezignan]; Jacques Colombies [Carcassonne], Roger Garnung [Bordeaux]; Georges Ribot [Carcassonne], Rene Segura [Carcassonne], Phillipe Dubie [Toulouse], George Ailleres [Toulouse, captain], Henri Marracq [St Gaudens] and Jean-Pierre Clar [Villeneuve]. The French substitutes were Andre Montcel [Marseille] and Henri Chamorin [Perpignan]. The referee was the redoubtable Mr Eric Clay of Rothwell and the gate was 10,650.

The British Rugby League had adopted the then new four tackle rule some months earlier but as the French were still playing under the old system of unlimited tackles, the British agreed to play under the old rule. With the French looking to add to their impressive recent results by achieving a sixth consecutive Test win, this game developed into a thrilling encounter. Pierre Lacaze dropped an early goal but Neil Fox had Clive Sullivan racing in for a fine unconverted try. Lacaze added another super drop goal and then kicked a long range penalty goal to give France a 6–3 lead. Britain regained their advantage with an Alan Hardisty special when he sliced through the home defence for a cracking solo try and Neil Fox added the extras. Fox again created a second unconverted try for Hardisty, but the French equalized when Andre Ferren strode to the posts after picking up a dropped ball, Lacaze converting.

After 75 minutes of play Lacaze appeared to have won the game for France when he struck a fantastic 50 yard drop goal, his third of the game, to give his side a 13–11 advantage. Neil Fox had other ideas as he took a wide Terry Fogerty pass and removed Guy Andrieu with a mighty hand off to release Clive Sullivan on the half way line. Using his phenomenal pace, Sullivan zoomed around two French cover tacklers, dispensed with the services of another by simply sliding into third gear, swerved infield to remove two further defenders, and raced to the posts for a brilliant match winning try, Neil Fox naturally obliged with the extra two points and Great Britain won in the final minute 16–13. The French supporters stood as one to applaud Clive Sullivan's breathtaking effort.

Frank returned to club football after doing his share of good work in the victory in France. Swinton beat Widnes at Station Road in the first round of the Challenge Cup 16–7 as the 'Chemics' hit a run of reverses with six defeats and two draws in the next eight games. Barrow, home and away, Leigh at home, Workington away, Warrington at home and, of course, Swinton in the cup were the defeats to go with the two draws, both 4 points all, against Rochdale Hornets away and Oldham at home.

Frank missed the Oldham draw as he was selected again for Great Britain the day after against the French at Central Park, Wigan. Surprisingly the hero of the win in Carcassonne, Clive Sullivan, was out of the return game. The selectors named five changes in the Great Britain side which was, Arthur Keegan [Hull FC]; Bill Burgess [Barrow], Frank Myler [Widnes], Neil Fox [Wakefield Trinity], Ken Senior [Huddersfield]; Alan Hardisty [Castleford, captain], Keith Hepworth [Castleford]; Mick Harrison [Hull FC], Don Close [Huddersfield], Cliff Watson [St Helens], Bob Irving [Oldham], Bill Bryant [Castleford] and Dave Robinson [Swinton]. The French, as was their way, made several changes to their back line. Ferren, Mantaulan, Andrieu and Colombies went out and in came Bruzy, Lecompte, Gruppi and Ourliac. The full side was Pierre Lacaze [Marseille]; Guy Bruzy [Perpignan], Jean-Pierre Lecompte [St Gaudens], Jacques Gruppi [Villenuve]; Jean-Claude Marty [Lezignan]; Andre Ourliac [Limoux], Roger Garnung [Bordeaux]; Serge Pialat [Cavaillon], Rene Segura [Carcassonne], Phillipe Dubie [Toulouse], Georges Ailleres [Toulouse, captain], Henri Maracq [St Gaudens] and Jean-Pierre Clar [Villeneuve]. The referee was Monsieur Georges Jameau of Marseille, and the gate was 7,448.

Compared to the previous meeting of the two sides the game was of no comparison. The first was a fine, constructive thriller, this one was a scrappy sort of a Test match. The major significance of the 80 minutes of football was the injuries to all three of the Castleford players. Keith Hepworth suffered a broken hand, Alan Hardisty picked up a back injury and, although he played throughout the game, it made him a passenger and Bill Bryant was knocked unconscious in a tackle and broke his leg when falling! Starting with some grand rugby, Britain shot into a lead through an Arthur Keegan try followed by an Alan Hardisty special touchdown and a Neil Fox goal. Pierre Lacaze landed two goals then converted a strong try by Jean-Pierre Clar to give the French a 9–8 advantage. Lacaze produced his usual drop goal bonanza by landing two early successes in the second half. Britain levelled matters with a great try involving handling by Neil Fox, Frank Myler, Alan Hardisty and Bill Bryant before Dave Robinson dived in for Neil Fox to convert. Almost immediately Bill Bryant was on one of his powerful runs when he was challenged by Jean-Pierre Clar. One writer described the incident thus, 'Clar went in very high and Bryant went out very cold'. The big Castleford forward fell awkwardly and suffered a badly broken leg.

Keith Hepworth, bravely attempting a last ditch tackle on Henri Marracq, failed to stop the Frenchman who registered a try and poor Keith retired with a broken hand. Britain now had 11 men and were in an impossible situation as Lacaze converted the Marracq try and similarly added to the late try scored by Jean-Pierre Lecompte to give France a rare 23–13 victory on British soil.

This international match against France in March 1967 would be the last game that Frank would play for Great Britain for over three years. Also, Frank was coming to the end of his playing term at Widnes. The 1966–67 season was coming to an end, Oldham and Blackpool Borough were both beaten away from home, but the final league game at St Helens finished 25–10 to Saints, leaving Widnes with the tough visit to Leeds at Headingley in the play offs, Leeds winning 27–8.

Unknown to Frank negotiations had been taking place for his

transfer to St Helens. Frank was completely unaware that talks were taking place between the two clubs. He says:

> I got home from work one evening to find a message asking me to contact Bill Johnson the Widnes RLC secretary. I phoned Bill who told me that St Helens RLC had made an offer. He asked me if I would come down to the club to discuss the situation.
>
> When I arrived at the club the Chairman Mr Devonald, along with Bill Johnson, sat me down to discuss the details of the St Helens offer. I was told that St Helens had offered Ray French and Dave Markey who were both forwards, as well as the sum of £6,000 for me to sign for them. Mr Devonald said that the committee had decided to accept the offer, if I agreed. This came as a complete shock to me: after all, I had served 12 years with the club. I asked if I could speak to St Helens, not knowing that Basil Lowe, the Saints secretary, was actually waiting in the next room.
>
> After being introduced to Mr Lowe, we sat down together to have a chat. The first question I asked him was, 'What position would I play?'
>
> He replied, 'Stand off half.' He then told me that the Saints team was one of the best, if not the best, in the league. The team consisted of Cliff Watson, Tommy Bishop, Kel Coslett, John Mantle, Frank Barrow, Tony Barrow, John Warlow, Bill Sayer, Billy Benyon, John Walsh, to mention a few.
>
> After some discussion with Mr Lowe, I returned to Mr Devonald and Mr Johnson. I asked them the reasons why Widnes were prepared to let me go. Mr Devonald said that the club needed forwards and in Ray French they were getting a current international. He also said that the £6,000 would help the Widnes club's finances. After hearing their reasons, I signed for St Helens. Later, Ray French proved what a good buy he was for the club.

But Frank did play three further games for Widnes before the deal was finalised, Swinton at home, Halifax away and his final game for Widnes was in the home defeat by Warrington on 28 August 1967. Frank made his St Helens debut in the centre on 1 September 1967 in the home win over Salford. Ray French made his Widnes debut on 9 September in the away defeat against Swinton.

It must have come as a shock to the Widnes supporters to find out that the club was losing its most treasured son! It had been way back on 27 December 1955 that the 17 year old youngster had recorded two tries in the home win against Liverpool City. He had gained selection 15 times for Great Britain, once for England and 15 times for Lancashire county as well as three representative games for various charities. He had played 365 games for Widnes, plus two games as substitute. Frank recorded 146 tries for the club, and kicked seven goals, in his truly wonderful record. The Widnes faithful must have wondered why on earth he was going. Sometimes a transfer to another club was taken out of a player's hands when a club came for a player and the two chairmen discussed a move before the player knew. This is what happened in Frank's case. Often a player asked for a move or a club came for him without his knowledge with a swap deal or just a cash offer.

What makes a player, who has given 12 seasons of loyal service to his home town team, decide to seek pastures greener? Could it be the lack of big cup finals at the club as, in Frank's case, only one serious winners' medal whilst at the club. Could it be the lack of regular winning pay packets? Or maybe as a regular in international football and returning from a recent three month tour with players from Saints, Leeds, Wigan, Swinton and Castleford, Frank may have considered that, at 28 years old, it was now or never if he intended to make a move to upgrade his medal collection. I doubt thinking that Widnes had no chance of winning cups ever entered Frank's mind, as his loyalty to the club never waned. But top Lancashire clubs of the time seemed always to be winning this and that and suddenly one of the biggest clubs was seriously interested in signing him. So the deal went through, and Frank Myler reversed his decision of 12 years ago and agreed to join St Helens.

12

PLAYING AT SAINTS AND BACK TO AUSTRALIA

Frank soon settled in at Knowsley Road and was quickly setting up a fine centre-wing partnership with the strong running Les Jones. After his Salford debut came the difficult almost 'derby' match against Liverpool City, away. Frank opened his try account for Saints in this win by 32–5 by crossing for one of his special tries. Three days later he was on his way up to Workington in Cumberland to play for Lancashire against the home county. This time Frank was awarded a great accolade for the county when he was appointed captain of the Lancashire county side for the first time. The Lancashire side was Frank Barrow [St Helens]; Bill Burgess [Barrow], Chris Hesketh [Salford], Frank Myler [St Helens], Brian Glover [Warrington]; Willie Aspinall [Warrington], Tommy Bishop [St Helens]; Albert Halsall [St Helens], Bob Burdell [Salford], Brian Brady [Warrington], Mark Sanderson [Barrow], Ken Parr [Warrington] and Ray Clarke [Warrington]. Lancashire's substitute was Doug Laughton [Wigan] who took over from Ray Clarke in the second half.

Cumberland, always a handful at home, went for a selection that would bring a patriotic appeal to the fiercely proud spectators. Their side was Paul Charlton [Workington Town]; Bob Wear [Barrow], Les Bettinson [Salford], John Coupe [Warrington], Keith Davies [Workington Town]; Phil Kitchen [Workington Town], Jack Newall [Workington Town]; Brian Edgar [Workington Town], Tom Hill [Whitehaven], Bill Martin [Workington Town], Rodney Smith [Workington Town], Bill Kirkbride [Workington Town] and Bill Pattinson [Workington Town]. The referee was Mr Henry Pearce of

Leeds and the attendance was almost 4,000. For Lancashire, Bill Burgess scored a brace of tries, Frank raced over for a super try, Tommy Bishop used his quick thinking and strength to register his try and Willie Aspinall's pace took him in for his score. Willie also landed two goals to give the Red Rose county their 19 points. Cumberland scored tries through Bob Wear and Les Bettinson. Aspinall and Bishop, Lancashire's half backs were in great form and this meant that Frank and co-centre Chris Hesketh had enormous freedom in midfield which they accepted with both hands. Lancashire were far better than their winning final score of 19–6 suggests.

Frank went back into club football, and three days after the Cumberland game he lined up against Leigh on the Saturday for his home debut. Again he treated the Saints supporters to a masterclass of centre play, scoring one try and having a hand in three more. The following Wednesday, Saints played in the second round of the Lancashire Cup away to Swinton. Saints had beaten Rochdale Hornets 7–4 at home in round one and the round two game at Station Road was just as hard with Saints having to defend well in a close 12–8 win. Frank was unable to play in any of Saints' successful Lancashire Cup games as he had played for Widnes in the first round and was therefore cup-tied for the remainder of that season's Lancashire Cup rounds. Saints went on to play Warrington in the final at Central Park, Wigan and drew 2 points each. The replay was held at Station Road, Swinton in early December because the Australian tourists were over here. Saints won the replay 13–10. This was the second time Frank had been unlucky in the County Cup as on his first season, Widnes reached the final only to lose to Leigh in October 1955 when Frank made his debut in December.

Frank's injury free period ended in the home win against Warrington on 27 September. He returned on 27 October in the 14–7 victory against Rochdale Hornets but was out of action again from that game until 16 December. He finally returned against Oldham at Knowsley Road for the win 10–2. One of the key games Frank missed was the excellent 8–4 win over the touring Australian side on 24 October. This was an unusually lean time for Saints in the cup stakes as the County Cup victory over Warrington was the lone success. Frank was in both the sides which completed the league double over the old enemy, Wigan. The first victory was on Boxing Day 1967 at Central Park, 16–10 and the second was on Good Friday 1968 when Wigan were beaten at Knowsley Road 24–13. The league season went satisfactorily with nine defeats and one draw, at Batley, 9 points all, in 34 games. The Challenge Cup run ended in round one with a shock 5–0 defeat at home by Huddersfield. In the Championship play offs, Halifax (31–2) and Warrington (20–0), were beaten at Knowsley Road, but Hull Kingston Rovers proved too good for Saints on the day and this season ended for them with a 23–10 defeat.

Frank did cross swords with the Aussies whilst playing for Lancashire on 11 October when, after recovering from his original injury against Warrington in September, he was declared fit to play against the Aussies. He lasted only until half time when the injury reoccurred. An added honour in this game was that he continued as captain of the side. The Lancashire county team in that game against Australia at Salford was Frank Barrow [St Helens]; Bill Burgess [Barrow], Chris Hesketh [Salford], Frank Myler [St Helens], Brian Glover [Warrington]; Willie Aspinall [Warrington], Tommy Bishop [St Helens]; Ken Halliwell [Barrow], Bob Burdell [Salford], Brian Brady [Warrington], Mark Sanderson [Barrow], Ken Parr [Warrington] and Ray Clarke [Warrington]. The two Lancashire substitutes, Stuart Whitehead [Salford] and Eddie Tees [Barrow] replaced Frank and Willie Aspinall at half time.

The Australians fielded Les Johns [Canterbury Bankstown]; Ken Irvine [North Sydney], Reg Gasnier [St George], Ron Saddler [Eastern Suburbs], Johnny King [St George]; Jackie Gleeson [Brisbane Brothers], Billy Smith [St George]; Dennis Manteit [Brisbane Brothers], Noel Kelly [Western Suburbs], Elton Rasmussen [St George], Ron Coote [South Sydney], Ron Lynch [Parramatta], Johnny Raper [St George]. The referee was Mr Appleyard of Leeds and the attendance was 9,369. Lancashire's only points in this hard game came from a penalty goal by Ken Halliwell. The Aussies scored 14 points in return through tries by Reg Gasnier and Johnny King with Les Johns kicking four goals. It was accepted as a brave effort by all the

Lancashire team.

The Australian tour had caused the inter-county championship to be extended, and the play off final was between Yorkshire and Lancashire, as both teams had beaten Cumberland. The play off was staged at Naughton Park, Widnes on 24 January 1968. Yorkshire wanted to take the championship and selected a side they thought good enough to beat Lancashire. It was Arthur Keegan [Hull FC]; Chris Young [Hull Kingston Rovers], Alan Burwell [Hull Kingston Rovers], Neil Fox [Wakefield Trinity], John Atkinson [Leeds]; Roger Millward [Hull Kingston Rovers], Barry Seabourne [Leeds]; Mick Clark [Leeds], Don Close [Huddersfield], Doug Walton [Castleford], Terry Ramshaw [Bradford Northern], Bill Ramsey [Leeds] and Terry Major [Hull Kingston Rovers]. The Yorkshire forward substitute was Alan Hepworth of Bradford Northern who replaced Terry Ramshaw in the second half.

Lancashire selected 'horses for courses' and produced a side which in fact was well balanced, Colin Tyrer [Wigan]; Bill Burgess [Barrow], Alan Buckley [Swinton], Frank Myler [St Helens], Brian Glover [Warrington]; Denis O'Neil [Widnes], Tommy Bishop [St Helens]; Ken Halliwell [Barrow], Bob Burdell [Salford], Geoff Fletcher [Oldham], Ray French [Widnes], Terry Fogerty [Wigan] and Doug Laughton [Wigan]. Their back substitute was Tommy Warburton [Oldham] who went on for Bill Burgess. The referee was Mr George Wilson of Dewsbury and 8,932 attended.

The game developed into a thriller with nothing between the teams. Frank made a superb try for Brian Glover with a break and well timed pass. But it was the tremendous pace of Denis O'Neil, with two fabulous tries, which killed the visitors. Both the Lancashire props, Ken Halliwell and Geoff Fletcher scored tries from excellent support play and Colin Tyrer tidied things up with four fine goals. Yorkshire were in the game right to the end and their tries came from some excellent attacking football. John Atkinson, Roger Millward and Terry Ramshaw scored good tries and Neil Fox added four goals.

The season 1968–69 promised much as St Helens had built up a fine, open football playing side. A long string of wins opened the league results, with Saints only losing at Leeds 20–13 in the third game of the season, before dropping another point in the 10 points all draw at Salford in early October. The quest for the Lancashire Cup began with a visit by Wigan to Knowsley Road. A fine 19–16 win gave Saints a trip to Widnes in round two. In another close game, St Helens fought their way through to a hard semi final with Leigh away. In the win at Widnes, Frank scored one of Saints' tries and it seemed strange for him to be scoring against Widnes after all the seasons he had spent there. Leigh were beaten 17–6 with Frank crossing again for a fine try. The following Saturday, Saints gained revenge against Leeds with a great 28–3 win at home. Oldham were Saints' opponents in the County Cup final but before that big game another trophy was on the go.

The BBC2 Floodlit Trophy started for Saints with the first round over two legs against Barrow. Saints won the first leg at home 21–5 and although losing the second leg at Craven Park 18–11, went through on a 39–16 aggregate win. They then beat Swinton 12–10 at Knowsley Road in a thriller before beating Hull FC 14–10 at home and Warrington, again at home, in the semi final. The final of the BBC2 Floodlit Trophy was between Wigan and St Helens at Central Park, Wigan. But before that came the Lancashire Cup final against Oldham at Wigan. Saints proved to be too quick and strong for brave Oldham and went on to lift the Lancashire Cup by a big 30–2 margin. Frank played in the centre and picked up his first major cup winners medal since Widnes's great win at Wembley in 1964. The gate in the County Cup final was 17,008. Seven weeks later on 17 December, Frank and his St Helens team mates were at Wigan again in the BBC2 Floodlit Trophy final. The pitch on that evening was, as one would expect, heavy with clinging mud! In a dour, unrelenting slog, Wigan came away with an exhausting 7–4 win before 13,479 spectators. Nine days later, on Boxing Day, Wigan came to Knowsley Road in the league but the game was abandoned at half time due to a frost-bitten hard pitch with Saints leading 11-3. It was replayed on 14 January when Saints eventually gained revenge with a 13–3 win.

In the play offs St Helens had the home advantage. They beat Keighley 25–7, then came Featherstone Rovers, a club with a tradition of being hard cup fighters. The Rovers went down heavily, with Frank playing really well and scoring two tries in the crushing 47–4 win for Saints. Into the final four teams for the championship and St Helens drew another rugged side in Castleford. The Lancashire League set up meant St Helens only played four Yorkshire clubs in the league, Leeds, Wakefield Trinity, Doncaster and Hull Kingston Rovers. Of the teams faced in the play offs, Keighley, Featherstone Rovers and Castleford were unknown quantities. Castleford however were a special team around this time, with Derek Edwards, Alan Hardisty, Keith Hepworth, Mal Reilly, Dennis Hartley, Brian Lockwood and a host of other good players. They came to St Helens, and outplayed Saints with a score of Saints 6 Castleford 18! Frank had a Lancashire Cup winners medal and a wonderful league and cup season with Saints having a record of played 50 (not including the abandoned Boxing Day match with Wigan), won 39, drawn 2, lost 9. Two hard to take defeats had come at the hands of Wigan in the muddy BBC2 Floodlit Trophy final and Warrington at Wilderspool in the third round of the Challenge Cup, when Saints had, for the better part of the game, outplayed Warrington, only to lose 4–2. St Helens had beaten Warrington twice in the league, 24–11 at home and 20–5 away, plus they'd scored a great win in the BBC2 Floodlit Trophy at home 29–6. The beauty of the Challenge Cup was seen in all its glory in Warrington's unexpected win.

Frank had made the transition from Widnes to Saint Helens with the ease that everyone expected. A supremely talented footballer, Frank fitted in well either at stand off half to Tommy Bishop at number seven or in the centre as partner to the excellent Les Jones. Saints also played a brand of rugby that suited Frank's game. He enjoyed stand off half far better than centre but being a centre in that star studied Saints team ensured a regular supply of the ball. Co-centres with Frank were Billy Benyon, Tony Barrow, John Walsh and Alan Whittle. The forward Frank rated for being able to supply him with passes was Kel Coslett who moved successfully from full back to loose forward and offered the perfect link between the big, mobile Saints pack and the quick, elusive three quarters on the outside. In Frank's first season at Saints he had the great wingman Tom van Vollenhoven in the centre with him but a defeat at Knowsley Road by Leeds saw the brilliant finisher, 'The Van', back on the wing the following weekend!

Recalling his early days with St Helens, Frank says:

Having had a reasonable start to my first season with St Helens, I looked forward to the 1969–70 season. During the summer of 1969 Tommy Bishop had gone to play in Australia, while Joe Coan had been replaced as coach by Cliff Evans during 1967–68. Saints had also signed on a young scrum half, Jeff Heaton, to replace Tommy Bishop. Cliff Evans was well respected in the game and had been coach at Swinton for a number of seasons. During that period Swinton won two league Championships and reached four Lancashire Cup finals.

My first conversation with Cliff was by phone. He asked me what I thought about Austin Rhodes, who had been with him at Swinton. I asked, 'Why? Is he available?' When Cliff replied that he was, I immediately said, 'Sign him.' Austin could play at any back position and excelled at all of them, plus he could also kick goals. He was a players' player.

Austin had started his career at St Helens, signing on when he was 16 years of age. He played his first first-team game at the age of 17 against Liverpool City on 28 March 1955. His international career began two years later when he was selected to play in the 1957 World Cup in Australia.

The very first time I played with Austin was in the 1960 World Cup. We were both selected to play in the final against Australia, a game we won 10–3. Austin kicked two goals. He played in full back position and I was at stand off half. It is always said within the game, 'If you need to know how good a player is, you need to have played with him not against him.' Austin's reading of a game was as good as it gets and knowing Austin would be on our side in the coming season could only enhance St Helens chances of winning some silverware.

So the 1969–70 season arrived, and with it the knowledge that this was another touring period. Frank, although playing as well as ever, would be 31 years old. He still had the yearning to go back to Australia and beat the old enemy in their own back yard. There were some dynamic youngsters pushing through in the three quarters, Chris Hesketh at Salford, Syd Hynes at Leeds, the excellent utility player, so important on tour, Mick Shoebottom of Leeds, Alan Hardisty at Castleford, Roger Millward at Hull Kingston Rovers and many more. Frank had captained Lancashire County twice in 1967 and had won the Cumberland game but lost as captain against the touring Aussies at Salford. So he did what he always did, put his head down, grafted for his club and hoped for the best!

That season, Frank's exploits, mainly at stand off, earned him an early call for Lancashire County. On 1 September Frank played against Maryport, the Cumberland junior club, who had fought their way into the first round draw of the County Cup. Frank recorded six tries against them in the 58–5 win for Saints. The call to the county side was to play against Cumberland at Workington in a side captained by Alex Murphy. Lancashire's selection was Ray Dutton [Widnes]; Bill Burgess [Salford], Chris Hesketh [Salford], Frank Myler [St Helens], Mike Murray [Barrow]; Alex Murphy [Leigh], Parry Gordon [Warrington]; John Stephens [Wigan], Kevin Ashcroft [Leigh], Mark Sanderson [Barrow], Bob Welding [Leigh], Dave Robinson [Swinton] and Doug Laughton [Wigan]. Dave Hill of Wigan was a second half substitute for Alex Murphy. Cumberland selected Paul Charlton [Workington Town]; Bob Wear [Warrington], Tony Colloby [Blackpool Borough], Ian Wright [Workington Town], Keith Davies [Workington Town]; Bob Ryan [Whitehaven], Harry Maddison [Whitehaven]; Harold McCourt [Workington Town], Howard Allen [Workington Town], Denis Martin [Workington Town], Eddie Bowman [Whitehaven], Tom Gainford [Whitehaven] and Bill Pattinson [Warrington]. Cumberland's substitutions were John Shimmings of Whitehaven for Ian Wright and John 'Spanky' McFarlane of Workington Town for Bill Pattinson. The referee was Mr Eric Clay, and the attendance was 2,148.

Alex Murphy led the way with three classical tries, with Parry Gordon, Dave Robinson and Doug Laughton adding one each. Ray

Dutton landed six fine goals to give Lancashire the win by 30–10. For Cumberland, Bob Ryan and Harry Maddison crossed for tries, and Tony Colloby kicked two goals.

Widnes knocked Saints out of the Lancashire Cup with a great 22–14 win at Naughton Park where, in the second game of the season, the Chemics also had administered a 17–5 defeat to the Saints. Castleford and Leeds both beat St Helens on their own grounds in early season and Salford's victory at The Willows inflicted the fifth defeat in 16 games. The BBC2 Floodlit Trophy began for Saints with a win at Swinton. The second round took Saints to Craven Park for a difficult game against Barrow and they came away with a hard fought 11–6 win. In the league, Saints lost away to Featherstone Rovers and on 9 December Frank was at stand off half in the third round of the BBC2 Floodlit Trophy when Saints went to Central Park to take on Wigan. The game ended as a 13–all draw. Saints suffered the ignominy of a 15–9 defeat at Knowsley Road two days later in the replay. Then on Boxing Day 1969 Saints went to Central Park again in the annual fixture. Turning on a brilliant performance, Saints beat Wigan by an amazing 53–11!

New Years Day 1970 saw Swinton earn a draw at Knowsley Road by 18 points each. In those first 21 league games, Saints lost six and drew one of their games. But they were out of two cups! Towards the end of March, Frank travelled to a meeting in Leigh with Mr Jack Harding. At that meeting Frank was invited to captain the 1970 Great Britain Lions tour to Australia and New Zealand with Mr Harding as tour Manager and Frank's old international mate, John Whiteley, as coach (combined with a number of other tour jobs).

The Challenge Cup began in early February, with St Helens taking on Bradford Northern at home. Saints went through 16–3. Bramley came next and again had to travel to Saints where Bramley lost 17–2. The draw for round three gave Saints an awkward cup tie at Doncaster on the tight little Tattersfield ground. With a 4 points all draw it is easy to see that that game could have gone either way but the replay at Knowsley Road saw Saints march into the semi final on a 36–0 ticket. Castleford were the current cup holders and had a young, sturdy, alert side. The semi final was played at Station Road, Swinton on 4 April and was attended by almost

19,000 spectators. The Saints team that day was Frank Barrow; Les Jones, John Walsh, Alan Whittle, Frank Wilson; Frank Myler, Jeff Heaton; Cliff Watson, Bill Sayer, Albert Halsall, Eric Chisnall, John Mantle and Kel Coslett. The two Saints substitutes were Eric Prescott and Graham Rees. This was a challenging cup semi final where neither side gave anything away. Castleford won the right to go back to Wembley for the second consecutive time by way of a 6–3 win, Les Jones scoring the Saints try.

The play offs brought Warrington to Knowsley Road and Saints marched on with a 36–8 win. They beat Leigh 16–5, then came a trip across the Pennines to Castleford in the championship semi final. A real crunch match occurred and at the final whistle it was 9 points all. Two days later came the replay, and no doubt Castleford had their minds on the Wembley cup final as Saints turned on the power with a fine 21–12 win to take them into the championship final against Leeds. They played the game at Odsal Stadium, Bradford and it was an excellent game to watch for the 26,358 spectators. Again Saints rose to the occasion, and with two Eric Prescott tries along with one each from Bill Sayer and John Walsh and goals from Kel Coslett (4) and John Walsh (2), they stormed home by 24–12. Frank had an outstanding game and was awarded the Harry Sunderland Trophy as the best player of the match.

Frank's story took another twist as he travelled once again across the world to take on the Aussies and Kiwis down under. This time he had a more significant role as he was the tour captain!

The full touring squad was Ray Dutton [Widnes], Terry Price [Bradford Northern], Derek Edwards [Castleford], John Atkinson [Leeds], Clive Sullivan [Hull FC], Alan Smith [Leeds], Mick Shoebottom [Leeds], Chris Hesketh [Salford], Syd Hynes [Leeds], Frank Myler [St Helens, captain], Alan Hardisty [Castleford], Roger Millward [Hull Kingston Rovers], Keith Hepworth [Castleford], Barry Seabourne [Leeds], Dave Chisnall [Leigh], Denis Hartley [Castleford], Cliff Watson [St Helens], Johnny Ward [Salford], Peter 'Flash' Flanagan [Hull Kingston Rovers], Tony Fisher [Bradford Northern], Jimmy Thompson [Featherstone Rovers], Phil Lowe [Hull Kingston Rovers], Bob Irving [Oldham], Dave Robinson [Wigan], Doug Laughton [Wigan] and Malcolm Reilly [Castleford].

13

THE MOST FAMOUS
OF TOURS

Frank explains the comradeship, the few disappointments, the laughs and the fantastic feeling of the successes of the famous 1970 tour.

What were my feelings as I stepped off the plane in May 1970 and onto the Australian soil for the second time? Certainly I knew that I did not want to be leaving at the end of July in the same way I had left four years before. I also felt a huge sense of responsibility. This feeling was so different to the responsibilities I had felt in 1966 when I had toured as just a player with a player's responsibilities. Now I was captain and although this team had a respected coach, John Whiteley, which we didn't have in 1966, I knew that on the field a hell of a lot would be resting both on my shoulders and on the shoulders of the other experienced tourists such as Cliff Watson.

I had a feeling of optimism when I looked at the potential of the squad of players selected. We had some fine youngsters who would benefit from this tour and I knew the calibre of Cliff Watson. He was a strong, fierce competitor who would act as a catalyst to the rest of the forwards. On the other hand, I was aware that a great player in England would not necessarily be a great player in Australia. The old saying on tour is that Australia either makes you or breaks you and it is true. The Australia tour breaks more than it makes. I remembered what had happened four years before and thought about all the things that could go wrong and of the great teams of the past that had not made it.

But I was still determined to do everything in my power to avoid those terrible feelings of failure.

The Australian team were a bit of an unknown quantity. Great Britain had not played them since 1968 in the World Cup and they had beaten us 25–10 in Sydney. We had only five survivors of that beaten team in our squad of 26 players so I thought we would have a few surprises up our sleeves for them, particularly with great prospects like Hynes, Reilly, Laughton, Thompson and Fisher.

The tour started well enough in the usual format of arriving in Darwin and working their way down the North East coast. The Northern Territory side were taken on in Darwin in the first game of the tour and it is worthwhile looking at the first team to represent Britain on the tour. The team was Price; Sullivan, Myler, Hesketh, Smith; Hardisty, Hepworth; Chisnall, Fisher, Ward, Lowe, Thompson and Reilly. Four substitutes were used, Atkinson, Millward, Irving and Robinson. A steady run out in the heat of Darwin ended in a good 35–12 first win. After that the travelling began! Game two took place in steaming hot Townsville against North Queensland, which, give or take a mile or two, was roughly 2,000km from Darwin. The changes made to the team for the second game were sizable: Dutton; Smith, Edwards, Hynes, Atkinson; Shoebottom, Seabourne; Watson, Flanagan, Hartley, Robinson, Lowe and Laughton, with Millward and Irving as subs.

As usual the North Queenslanders gave it their all with some tough tackling to say this was no mere outback district. But the tourists stuck at it and a 23–20 victory was the hard fought outcome. From there it was down the coast to Rockhampton for a game against the Central Queensland district which Britain won 30–2. Then the tourists went inland for the next game at Wondai where they played Wide Bay at the foot of The Great Dividing Range, more or less half way between Rockhampton and Brisbane. A 45–7 win put the squad in good heart as two days later came the toughest game, on paper, of the opening tour games. This was against Queensland in Brisbane in front of the biggest attendance so far on the tour, 17,071. To put the early part of the tour into perspective, the team played the first game at Darwin on 22 May and they played the Queensland game on 30 May. This meant that not only had the squad travelled every other day down the coast, they had also played five games in eight days, Bob Irving involved in all five games. The tourists breezed through the Queensland game to win 32–7. Despite being unbeaten, Frank was not at ease with the type of matches in the build up to the first Test.

He recollects,

We had started very well running up high scores against far weaker tackling country sides than we would encounter in the Tests. Whilst this might have been a good way to boost confidence, I was not convinced that this was the best way of preparing for a Test match against Australia. No matter what you do, and try as you may to eliminate this from your team, complacency and slackness creep into your thinking and your tactics, both in defence and attack.

Against the district sides you have too much time and space in which to work. Both these aspects are denied in Test football. Anyone who has ever had experience in Test class games will tell you that their first impression of Test football is of the tremendous speed with which things happen. Even the greatest players have had to adjust to the speed of these matches. The Aussie press didn't help either. On the strength of our performances in the country games against the weak up country teams in Northern Territories and Queensland, they made us favourites. They were either very naïve or treacherously clever to give us a false sense of our own ability.

It was 6 June 1970 and the team were at Lang Park, Brisbane. If John Whitely was right the Aussies would set about his side with determined defence and powerful running from the first whistle to make an early show against the tourists. The Great Britain team was Terry Price [Bradford Northern]; Clive Sullivan [Hull FC], Frank Myler [St Helens, captain], Mick Shoebottom [Leeds], John Atkinson [Leeds];

Alan Hardisty [Castleford], Keith Hepworth [Castleford]; Dave Chisnall [Leigh], Peter Flanagan [Hull Kingston Rovers], Cliff Watson [St Helens], Dave Robinson [Wigan], Doug Laughton [Wigan] and Malcolm Reilly [Castleford]. The British subs were Roger Millward [Hull Kingston Rovers] and Bob Irving [Oldham]. The Aussies had selected a hard tackling side with the fearsome Arthur Beetson in the second row. The full side was, Graeme Langlands [St George]; Johnny King [St George], John McDonald [Manly], Johnny Brass [Eastern Suburbs], the Rev John Cootes [Wests, Newcastle]; Phil Hawthorne [St George], Billy Smith [St George]; John Wittenberg [St George], Elwyn Walters [South Sydney], Jim Morgan [Eastern Suburbs], Arthur Beetson [Balmain], Ron Lynch [Parramatta] and Ron Coote [South Sydney]. Their subs were Bob Thompson [Wests, Brisbane] and Col Weiss [Bundaberg]. The referee was Mr Don Lancashire of New South Wales and the attendance at Lang Park was 42,807.

The Australians hit Great Britain like a hurricane, and the wind behind the Aussie sail was Arthur Beetson who produced a blinder of a game. There were several clashes between the players and Jim Morgan had his nose broken. Ron Lynch accidentally broke his cheekbone in a collision with Beetson. After 20 minutes, Australia were ahead from three Langland's penalty goals, 6–0, then Morgan intercepted a pass and raced over for Langlands to convert from the touchline. Cliff Watson burst over for a try, Terry Price converting but Phil Hawthorn landed the first of his two drop goals to send the Aussies in at half time 13–5 in front.

John McDonald collected a Hawthorne kick through to crash over, Langlands adding the extras only two minutes into the second half. Then shortly afterwards Johnny King showed his pace in scoring a beauty, goaled by Langlands. Peter Flanagan's try and a Terry Price penalty goal raised hopes, but another Morgan try and two goals by Langlands took the score to Australia 30 Great Britain 10. Doug Laughton romped in for a fine try which Terry Price converted but Langlands added a penalty goal and converted King's final try. The final score was Australia 37 Great Britain 15.

Frank continues:

After 20 minutes of that first Test we were 11 points down. I can remember the shell shocked faces of Dave Chisnall, Malcolm Reilly, Doug Laughton and Terry Price as we lined up under the posts after an Aussie try. None of the players had played in a Test match before and they were swept off their feet by the speed and intensity of the Aussies' attacks. We tried to fight back but the game had gone away from us. The Aussies were playing with all the confidence and verve that this kind of start to a game gives you. They were doing nothing out of the ordinary, just using direct, forceful straight running, supporting excellently, and they clicked into that typical Aussie style you see when they are on top.

When we had the ball we made too many handling errors. These errors were forced upon us by Australia's ultra strong tackling and their defence was ferocious. We had not come across anything like this at all on the tour so far. We went through the motions of shaking hands and as we trooped off the pitch at Lang Park, into the changing rooms, the lighting system failed! To me that felt most appropriate. The lights had gone out for me too. In my first Test as tour captain, a far superior side crushed us on the day and my high hopes of only two hours ago lay in ruins. There was a heavy depressive feeling throughout the dressing room, a feeling of black despair and total disappointment. It was written in the squad's faces and one could hear it in their voices.

Now was the time for a good manager to show his worth and our manager did just that. The atmosphere on the bus back to the hotel was dreadful and just as bad on arriving at our hotel. We all felt low. Our manager, Jack Harding, and our coach, John Whiteley, acted as if we had just hammered the Aussies. We had one hell of a party that night. There was an old fashioned jukebox on the ground floor and we carried it up into the dining room, the beer flowed and we all gradually recovered our good spirits and began laughing and joking again. If any of the press boys had seen us they would have had a field day. I could see the headlines, 'Poms go raving Bonkers'. But it was brilliant psychology by Jack

Frank Barton's 'Sketchbook'

No. 1: FRANK MYLER (Widnes)

In cartoon in the sixties

League Championship winners 1970 St Helens v Leeds (Bradford)

1970 Great Britain portrait

Great Britain 1970 World Cup squad at Leeds RLFC, Headingley

1970 Lions squad at Leeds RLFC, Headingley

1970 Ashes victory

Getting a grip on Father Coote in the 1970 final Test at Sydney Cricket Ground

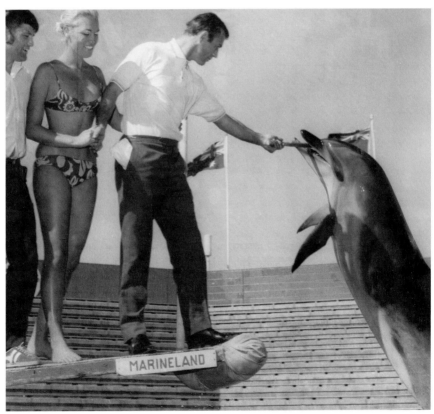

Feeding the dolphins with Flash Flanagan in Queensland

Sydney Cricket Ground 1970, players from left to right, David Chisnall, Chris Hesketh and Barry Seabournse

Relaxing the day before the final Test match on the golf course with Australian immigrant Charlie Rennilson, an ex Great Britain and Halifax player

Pictured (from left to right) with, among others, Bill Buckley (Chairman, Australian Rugby League), Jack Harding (Great Britain tour manager) and Father Coote (Australian player)

Widnes 1977–78 team, Club Championship winners, Lancashire cup

1984 Australia and New Zealand tour team

2005 reunion at Widnes Golf Club with Billy Boston (Wigan and Great Britain), Graham Langlands (Australian Test player) and Jim Mills (Widnes and Great Britain)

and John. We needed an immediate solution to stop us brooding about what had happened that afternoon.

The hotel we stayed at in Brisbane was the perfect place for such a shindig. We couldn't do much harm to a place like that. I know the public think that touring teams always stay in five star hotels with caviar and champagne on draught in each bedroom. I wish they could have seen the Railway Hotel in Brisbane. It has probably been pulled down by now but when we first saw it in 1970 we couldn't believe our eyes! The only covering on the floors was a faded lino which looked as if it had been down since Captain Cook's day. The furniture was old Victorian, and all the rooms were decorated in the same dirty brown colour. The facilities weren't that hot either. Every day, when we had been out on the training pitch in the local park, we came back to the hotel for our shower. Obviously in a place as old as this there were no private shower cubicles. The shower area was in this big sort of wash room with the showers in an open communal area at the end of the room. The old dear who was employed to mop the place out and clean this room always seemed to do it just once a day, the very time all the lads were back from training and taking their shower! She must have seen some sights as she shuffled around amongst us mopping up.

There were just 14 days between the first and second Test matches. The Great Britain tourists had four fixtures to play on their way down from Brisbane to Sydney, two of them still in Queensland. Toowoomba was the first and the opposition was the Toowoomba district side. This game was played the day after the Test match and three of the squad, Mick Shoebottom, Doug Laughton and Frank Myler played in the two games. The result was another fine 37–13 win considering the good quality of the opposition. Back across to Brisbane to play a traditional fixture against the Brisbane league side. Another win for the British by 28–7 saw the team say farewell to the Railway Hotel, but not before the final practical 'animal' joke was played on—you've guessed it—Peter 'Flash' Flanagan. Frank retold the story as follows:

The dining room in the Railway Hotel was no better than anywhere else in the place. One day the squad were eating their dinner when suddenly an enormous rat shot out and scuttled across the floor of the dining room in full view! Flash Flanagan was definitely not amused. If there was anything he hated more than snakes or birds, it was rats and I think he had an idea, even then, what was coming! Perhaps he remembered some of the tricks we played on him on the 1966 tour. He wasn't wrong either. We borrowed some rat traps and set them out. On checking the traps later, we found we had caught a huge rat (dead of course). A dead or alive rat would have made no difference to Flash. He had heard the rumours about the rat traps and figured he would be under attack that evening. Flash and his roommate Mick Shoebottom dashed upstairs and barricaded their room. They pulled the big old wardrobe against the door, pushed their beds against it and then put their shoulders against the beds ready for the inevitable invasion.

Unfortunately they both had missed the one chink in the room's armour, the fanlight above their door! I climbed up onto someone's shoulders and gently eased open the fanlight. I then swung the dead rat by the tail and lobbed it like a grenade into the fanlight. Poor old Flash passed away not too long ago but I know he fathomed out who was the rat culprit. He wasn't too bad at practical jokes himself and he played a beauty on us not long after. In Sydney, a group of us went to a large, modern swimming pool with several tiers of diving boards. The top board instilled one with vertigo by just looking down at the water from it. A couple of us had been to the top to have a look but there was no way I was either diving or jumping from that height, so we came down again via the ladders. Flash let it be known that he was going up to have a look. Up he went with Cliff Watson and me creeping up the ladder behind him. Flash got to the end of the board and turned to see us both in threatening mode, obviously intent on throwing him in! I will never know how he managed it but as we lunged to grab him he dropped to his knees and wiggled between our legs.

Cliff and I lost our balance and fell headlong, screaming from the top board into the pool. Nice one Flash!

On 13 June the tourists played in a fixture that always was as hard as a Test match. This was against New South Wales at the Sydney Cricket Ground. The New South Wales side was virtually a Test team. Many good judges consider this performance by the tourists to be the deciding game of the whole tour. Frank Myler's attitude in this game and his determination to captain a successful tour shone like a beacon and his astute knowledge of the game, his skilful play and his tactical know how guided the team in pulling back a substantial deficit to earn a great draw against this Test strength outfit. The British side which played New South Wales was Edwards; Sullivan, Hynes, Myler, Atkinson; Millward, Hepworth; Watson, Fisher, Hartley, Thompson, Lowe and Laughton. Atkinson, Hynes and Laughton scored the side's three tries with Millward kicking four goals. Because of the wonderful lead by Frank in this New South Wales game and the spirit the side showed in coming back against all the odds, some of the more experienced Aussie writers began to look at the squad from a different view point. 'Now then,' they said, 'these Poms can play a bit!' and suddenly realised that if given the chance, they could take Australia all the way.

The last game before the vital second Test was down near the capital of Australia, Canberra at Queanbeyan on 14 June. Two players only started in this game as well as in the crucial second Test, Alan Smith and Jim Thompson. The tourists won the game in Queanbeyan against Monaro 34–11.

On 20 June dawned the second Test day. The Aussies declared their side early in the week consisting of Ray Laird [Mackay]; Johnny King [St George], John McDonald [Manly], Johnny Brass [Eastern Suburbs], Rev. John Cootes [West's, Newcastle]; Phil Hawthorne [St George], Billy Smith [St George]; John Wittenberg [St George], Brian Fitzsimmons [Townsville], John Sattler [South Sydney captain], Ron Coote [South Sydney], Arthur Beetson [Balmain], Col Weiss [Bundaberg], and their subs were Bobby Fulton [Manly] and Ron

Costello [Canterbury-Bankstown]. The Aussies had several changes forced upon them, Langlands, Morgan and Lynch were all out injured and replaced by Laird, Sattler and a positional change with Coote moving up from loose forward. Walters was replaced by Fitzsimmon at hooker and Weiss came in from sub forward to take Cootes' place. The interesting choice was the retained selection of the Rev. John Cootes, a Catholic priest on the wing.

The Great Britain team selection was explained by Frank:

For the second Test we made a number of team changes. Curiously we had three full backs with us on tour but there was no trouble selecting the full back, Derek Edwards was the obvious choice as Ray Dutton had dislocated his shoulder, and Terry Price was out injured. For all the other positions we simply selected the men in form. This meant that the star of the 1966 tour, Alan Hardisty was out, as the selection at stand off was Roger Millward who had earned his promotion on the strengths of some outstanding country games. The same was true for Alan Smith and Syd Hynes in the backs and Denis Hartley, Tony Fisher and Jimmy Thompson in the pack. Jimmy Thompson was only 19 years old. There were no computers in those days to tell you who had made most tackles in a game. No one needed a computer when Jimmy was playing. He had an incredible appetite for work on the field, covering mile after mile without ever seeming to tire. That is the sort of lad he is. When it was decided that he was the obvious choice for one of the second row positions, we decided to give him a rest from a mid week game as he had played in every game, except the first Test, on the tour. When he found out he was not playing in the Wednesday game, he came up to me and asked, privately, what he had done wrong to be dropped! That's the sort of forward you need in Australia!

The British team was Derek Edwards [Castleford]; Alan Smith [Leeds], Syd Hynes [Leeds], Frank Myler [St Helens, captain], John Atkinson [Leeds]; Roger Millward [Hull Kingston Rovers], Keith Hepworth

[Castleford]; Dennis Hartley [Castleford], Tony Fisher [Bradford Northern], Cliff Watson [St Helens], Doug Laughton [Wigan], Jimmy Thompson [Featherstone Rovers] and Malcolm Reilly [Castleford]. The two subs were Mick Shoebottom [Leeds] and Bob Irving [Oldham]. The referee was Mr Don Lancashire of New South Wales, and the attendance was 60,962.

This Great Britain side shook the Australians to the core. The British pack completely dominated the Aussie six with Reilly, Laughton, Fisher, Thompson, Watson and Hartley looking bigger and playing bigger than their opponents. Reilly was unbelievably physical and mobile and his kicking game caught the Aussies out more than once. Fisher, Hartley and Watson were the afraid-of-nothing trio of marauders who stole into home territory with foraging runs and brutal defence. The Aussie crowd knew a good footballer when they saw one and they envied the copybook midfield tackling of Thompson and his breathtaking cover hits. The pace, power and running ability of Laughton and Reilly also shone through as the back row forwards revealed their full potential to the Aussie crowd.

Indeed Great Britain gave Australia a masterclass on how to win Test matches by intelligent forward play making room for their backs to entertain. Roger Millward was the revelation behind his pack going forward, registering two tries and kicking seven goals in the match. John Atkinson used his electric pace to score a try and late in the game the crowd cheered Tony Fisher's 30 yard try, even though he had an injured leg! Syd Hynes was unlucky in that he dropped a fine goal but copped a beauty from Arthur Beetson two minutes later which removed two of his teeth. Syd retaliated and Mr Lancashire unbelievably sent him off without even giving Arthur a caution! The newspapers bitterly complained about the persistent offside tactics by the Brits as well as their consistently rough play. Now there's a change! Johnny King finally managed to cross for a try and John McDonald and Phil Hawthorne landed goals to give the Aussies 7 points but Frank Myler's boys scored 28 points in a turn up for the books.

Frank, Jack Harding, John Whiteley and the rest of the squad were delighted. Frank recalls his thoughts at key moments of the game:

We ran out onto the field at the Sydney Cricket Ground knowing that this was the crucial game of the tour. If we lost this one, even narrowly, the tour was as good as over and we would go down in the record books as just another bunch of failures. But there were no failures that afternoon. The Aussie forwards could make no headway against a pack which contained six of the best tacklers you could ever hope to see. Our scrum half, Keith Hepworth, was like a seventh forward member of this formidable pack and if the Aussies tried to move the ball wide they found our backs were just as good at knocking them over as our forwards were. I particularly remember several highly damaging crash tackles brought off in potentially dangerous situations by Alan Smith the Leeds wingman. He reminded me of Billy Boston at his best as he shot in from his wing position with perfect timing so that the Aussie centre received the ball and a bone crushing tackle simultaneously.

Roger Millward gave an outstanding performance and not only tackled with great determination but also equalled the points scoring record against the Australians in a Test match with two tries and seven goals. Although Roger gets my vote for the best all round stand off of all time, it would be wrong to single out any individual in a match like this. This was a triumph for teamwork and team spirit. We were the masters of Australia in every department and, though no Australian team ever gives up, the writing was on the wall for them well before half time. It was particularly satisfying for us to beat them by almost the same margin that they humiliated us by only two weeks before up in Queensland. This time the Australians trudged wearily off the field with dispirited faces and the Aussies were the ones who had to repair their shattered morale ready for the deciding Test in two weeks time at Sydney Cricket Ground.

Even though we won this game almost as we liked, one refereeing decision could have been fatal to us in a closer match. In the second half, our centre Syd Hynes clashed with the fearsome Aussie forward, Arthur Beetson. Naturally Syd came off the worse. Big Artie had knocked Syd unconscious and the poor lad was minus two teeth! The referee, Mr Lancashire rushed to the scene of the crime and blew his whistle frantically. All the British players expected the referee to send off Beetson but we should have known better. The referee pointed to the dressing room and sent off Syd Hynes!

So we had levelled up the series to one Test all. The team spirit was high and we were all on this tour as we had been from day one, together! The jokes and great banter continued as we prepared for the four games before the vitally important final Test. We didn't joke around all the time however. As a senior player or coach you have to realise when to pull back from the mickey-taking and extend a little sympathy now and again.

Often on tour there are youngsters, teenagers sometimes, who are uprooted from their little Cumberland, Lancashire or Yorkshire villages to the other side of the world. They well may be hard as nails rugby players on the outside but that does not mean they can cope with the break from everything that is familiar and dear to them back home. Home-sickness can be a problem for some players. I have had vulnerable men eager for me to read love letters from their sweethearts or show me photographs of sweet little blondes or brunettes from Wigan, or Halifax or Oswaldtwistle! At first I used to react in the usual crude way that you may expect from a hardened rugby league pro. I would also make jokes about the pictures I was being shown. But I soon realised that there was no fun in taking the mickey out of someone who can't get his own back and it dawned on me that as coach or captain there are some things you can't joke about to some people.

By the time I did become a coach I think I got it just about right. You don't necessarily expect to become a nursemaid or a substitute father when you become captain or coach of the Great Britain rugby league team.

The trip to Bathurst to play the Western Division was the first journey the day after the second Test. Alan Smith doubled up from the Test match to play in the centre and John Atkinson, Dennis Hartley and that workaholic Jimmy Thompson also donned the jersey again to play, Frank Myler and Cliff Watson subbed in the 40–11 win.

The tour fixtures this time included a game at Cronulla against a side chosen from amongst the best young players operating in the Sydney league. They played under the title of the Sydney Colts. Young, fast and very fit, these young men were trying to make a name for themselves. In a physical game the Colts pulled no punches but with the British backs on top form and Syd Hynes going in for his second hat trick of tries on this tour, Britain came out on top 26–7 with a healthy crowd of just over 14,000 watching.

As the tour ran towards the final matches, it highlighted the whole question of tour managers and coaches. Just as there is no substitute for experience on the part of players, nor is there a substitute for experience on the part of people running a tour party. They have to know the ropes. If your manager is too weak or too gentlemanly, those bloody Aussies will put one over on you sooner or later. Your manager is your General, both in the propaganda war and in the whole strategy of the campaign. He has to be firmly in control of his men, yet gain their respect and trust. If he does not know what is involved in a long tour of Australia he could easily be out-manoeuvred by the enemy. Even the best of them can be caught out!

What sounds friendlier than a relaxing day's coach trip to the beautiful Snowy Mountains? It seemed the perfect way to recharge our batteries before the rigours of the final Test match. But when we fell for this one in 1970, the trip having been arranged for us by the Australian authorities, we found it was just the opposite! We were cramped on that coach for about 10 hours and damn near stranded up there. The coach driver had to put a chain on his wheels to get sufficient grip on the treacherous road surface before he could get us down again. The snow may be a curiosity to the Aussies but we see enough of it back home.

Between the wars it became the practice to send out an assistant manager with an experienced one so that there was a continuity of people with experience of the difficult job of managing a tour party. But after 1948, some people without any knowledge of touring conditions were sent out. It seems that Eddie Waring ran some of the tours. Eddie was a journalist whose main loyalty was to his newspaper that paid his wages. Rugby league players have to serve an apprenticeship, it is just as important that managers should do the same. After all what is the point of a good army without a good general?

Although most of the public attention is naturally centred on the Test matches and the games against the bigger divisional sides, the mid-week 'country' games are an important element in any tour. For the half of the party who don't command a regular Test place, the country games are the bread and butter of the whole tour. On all the tours I went on there were no bad feelings about playing in these games, although I've heard there was some animosity on other tours. Such was the spirit on the 1970 tour that there were no Ham'n'eggers. Amazingly, every player on that tour played in a Test match.

Almost all the 'country' games meant a plane trip out from one or the other of our main bases, either Brisbane or Sydney. Not all the touring party travelled: we usually sent 15 or 16 players to the game, and the remainder stayed in the hotel. This cut down the stress of every player suffering a plane journey and other travelling. It's difficult to say what playing in country games feels like. In one sense it is easier as the team does not meet the cream of Australian players. On the other hand country games can be just as hard as the showpiece games.

Take a couple of games from the 1970 tour as an example. One minor game in Ipswich was just another country game. We sent the usual number of players to this game and I was one of those players. The plane touched down in bright sunshine on the grass strip that was the only airport that this little township boasted. We landed to be welcomed by the most wonderful sight.

All the school children from miles around had gathered on the strip to welcome us in two lines forming a guard of honour which applauded us all the way down the line. For a few hours, those of us privileged to play in this game were treated like kings! It was the biggest event of the year for the people living in the remote district of Queensland. The last touring team to play there was in 1958, before many of the delighted children were born. It was a huge festival for them and some spectators had travelled hundreds of miles from far off sheep stations or farms, just for the pleasure of watching us play. It made us feel like ambassadors for our country. That was the nice side of travelling to country games!

Just before the deciding Test match in Sydney, we were due to play a country side coached by the famous former international player, Arthur Summons. Jack, John and I talked at length about the side that would play in this game. On one hand we wanted to win this game, just as we wanted to win every game on tour, as a defeat may well boost the morale of the Aussies in the crucial final Test. On the other hand we knew we would be in for a difficult game and could not risk injuries to our key players, or the likely possibility of having anyone sent off. This would mean suspensions, again affecting the availability of men for the Test match. It was tricky to decide what to do. Should we pick a strong side and go all out for a convincing victory? Or should I keep all our likely Test men back and risk losing our unbeaten run in these country games? It was a difficult choice but in the end we took the half way course and selected just six Test players.

We talked over our game plan and decided that the key words in our approach to this game would be discipline and restraint. Again we were certain that they would hit us hard and often and if we retaliated it could cause wholesale sending offs with the possibility of losing players for the Test match. We would obviously play right into the Aussies' hands if we gave them chance to suspend any of our key players. If that happened then it could break the whole success of the tour. So this was no ordinary run of the mill country game.

Straight from the kick off all our worst fears were justified. They hit us with everything but the kitchen sink. They were quite a good side anyway and what little they lacked in skill, they made up for in physical force. It was a game with a lot of dirt, elbows and punches and in the middle of all this mayhem we had our hands tied, as we had to play with absolute total restraint. We could make no retaliation nor could we utter a whisper of complaint. This game was played at Wagga Wagga against the Riverina district and 11,000 attended. We scraped home by 12–11—the closest of scores. But we had a price to pay. I was lucky as my only injury was a head wound that required four stitches but Derek Edwards was mauled so badly that his tour was finished! The team that did so well for our country that day was Edwards; Smith, Myler, Price, Atkinson; Hardisty, Shoebottom; Ward, Flanagan, Chisnall, Thompson, Irving and Lowe, with Hepworth and Hartley as subs. Peter Flanagan and John Atkinson scored our tries and Terry Price kicked three goals. The Aussie tactics were obvious, as six days later we played Australia at Sydney Cricket Ground. If we had lost a player through being sent off, rest assured that player would not have been available for this vital final Test.

Saturday 4 July 1970 was a date branded into the hearts of all Great Britain supporters! It was the day our tourists covered themselves with glory. In some respects the tourists were given a favour by Arthur Summons and his Riverina team with the harsh and often dirty tactics handed out as it served to remind the touring squad just what would be needed in this crucial encounter. The pitch at the Cricket Ground was hard and fast. The two teams lined up as follows: Great Britain, Mick Shoebottom [Leeds]; Alan Smith [Leeds], Syd Hynes [Leeds], Frank Myler [St Helens, captain], John Atkinson [Leeds]; Roger Millward [Hull Kingston Rovers], Keith Hepworth [Castleford]; Denis Hartley [Castleford], Tony Fisher [Bradford Northern], Cliff Watson [St Helens], Doug Laughton [Wigan], Jimmy Thompson [Featherstone

Rovers] and Malcolm Reilly [Castleford]. The British subs were Alan Hardisty [Castleford] and Bob Irving [Oldham]. The Aussies fielded Allan McKean [Eastern Suburbs]; John McDonald [Manly], Bobby Fulton [Manly], Johnny Brass [Eastern Suburbs], Johnny King [St George]; Phil Hawthorne [St George, captain], Bob Grant [South Sydney]; Jim Morgan [Eastern Suburbs], Elwyn Walters [South Sydney], Arthur Beetson [Balmain], Bob McCarthy [South Sydney], Ron Costello [Canterbury Bankstown] and Ron Coote [South Sydney]. The two Aussie subs were Graeme Lye [Parramatta] and Col Weiss [Bundaberg].

Rugby league historian Robert Gate describes this game as 'a superb performance in winning back the Ashes Cup, alas, unless things change we will never win it again! Frank Myler's team were miles too good for Australia with the four point margin of their victory being a total travesty'. And Great Britain did win the Ashes in style scoring five tries to one. The reason for the closeness of the score was a great goal kicking exhibition by Allan McKean, on debut for the Kangaroos, who landed seven glorious goals. Brilliant as the goal kicking by McKean was, it was certainly helped by some strange decisions from Mr Don Lancashire of New South Wales who awarded 15 penalties against the Lions whilst awarding only eight to the tourists. McKean had kicked goals in the second, sixth and 11th minutes, and Roger Millward answered with a ninth minute penalty. Then Denis Hartley charged down a McKean clearing kick, collected the bounce and set sail for the Aussie line some 30 yards away. The big prop would not be caught and swept triumphantly over the line for Roger Millward to convert. Great Britain went in at half time with a 7–6 lead.

John Atkinson timed an intercepted pass from Arthur Beetson and sped away for a great try, and within two minutes Syd Hynes gathered a super Malcolm Reilly grubber kick through to score, Roger Millward converting. McKean landed three further 'gift' penalty goals, but Mick Shoebottom surged through on a magnificent run to send John Atkinson in, and Britain led 18–12. Arthur Beetson was sent off for an attack on his old enemy Cliff Watson but a try by Bob McCarthy and another goal by McKean made it 18–17 to the tourists. Just before the end Malcolm Reilly scattered the Aussie defence and put Doug Laughton through. He served Roger Millward with a pass from 40 yards out and Roger's pace did the rest as he zoomed over in the corner for the absolute winner to give Britain the Ashes by 21–17.

Frank remembers the final game in Australia and just a few of the incidents on this action packed tour:

We played the last game in Australia at Wollongong which was a notorious graveyard for touring teams of the past. After the brutal final Test we had only 12 fully fit players out of our 26 tourists. But to turn out a team containing all 12 fully fit men would mean that some of them would have to play well out of their normal position. Some of us nursing minor injuries had to hold our hands up and play. We knew in advance that the game would follow the usual pattern of games against touring sides with the home team trying to intimidate us with strong arm tactics from the start in the hope of knocking us off our stride. This time though we had nothing to lose as we remembered the game at Wagga Wagga against Riverina and all the stick we had to take because of the Test match being so close! This time we hit them with everything we had straight from the kick off. This game was played the day after the final Test match, on 5 July and our team was, Shoebottom; Smith, Hynes, Myler, Atkinson; Millward, Seabourne; Hartley, Fisher, Watson, Robinson, Thompson and Reilly.

For 20 minutes the Third World War was fought on that pitch. At the end of that time the referee called the two captains together and suggested a truce. I think he was worried that the Wollongong hospital wouldn't be able to cope! From that moment the rough stuff eased, we could concentrate on playing rugby and we went on to win 24–11. This meant that we had lost only one game in Australia, the first Test match and drawn one game against New South Wales. It was a satisfying feeling!

The British sporting journalists travelled about with the teams on tour and became well known to the players. We normally had good reports from them in coverage of games played. Not that it stopped them from slating us when we played badly but that seemed fair enough. Rugby league is big news in Australia though and this means that any tourist has to be wary of the Sydney gutter press. They will pounce on any suspected weakness or minor scandal and blow it up out of all proportion.

Frank still has a vivid recollection of that final Test in Sydney:

Our confidence was sky high for the crucial final Test. We produced a magnificent tour with just the one defeat in the first Test and the draw against New South Wales. The bright aspect was that we were getting better each game we played because of the good reaction among players on the field plus the excellent spirit of cooperation and common purpose within the squad. The Aussies were worried as all the newspapers tipped us to beat them in the decider. The writers were upset with the Aussie team selection and, as usual, had a downer on the selectors. We didn't pay much attention to that as we had seen it all before. We went into the first Test thinking we would win easily and caught a cold. Despite being confident, we cut out any complacency and over confidence as we knew strange things happen in rugby league.

    The team picked itself! Only an idiot would have dropped any of the players who had done so well in that middle Test. The exception was at full back. None of our regular full backs, Terry Price, Derek Edward or Ray Dutton, were fit to play. We had, of course, a fine young utility player who rose to the occasion brilliantly, Mick Shoebottom. He became our third full back in three Test matches and he did an excellent job. The game went according to plan, except for one aspect which we had no control over. That was the referee. We were the far superior team on the day. Our defence was as outstanding as it had been in the middle Test match and Roger Millward displayed sensational attacking. But time after time we were frustrated by the whistle. Mr

Lancashire gave a seemingly unending stream of penalties against us, not only breaking up our rhythm of play but also allowing Australia to keep in striking distance of us through the boot of Allan McKean who landed seven goals, six of them from penalty kicks.

Although the final score was 21–17, I think we were 40 points better than them on the day rather than four points better! I can understand a referee in a country game leaning towards the home side when tourists are murdering them by 50 or 60 points. But for a referee in a Test match to allow the slightest bias to either team is disgraceful. What credit or pleasure can anyone get by winning a game in such a way?

Many things happen in a Test match that spectators don't notice as they are so engrossed in the game. There was one incident in the final Test where the referee had no option but to send off the Australian star player, Arthur Beetson. Big Arty had become increasingly frustrated by our clear cut superiority as far a rugby skills were concerned. He started to mix it in the second half. On one occasion, Cliff Watson and I tackled him. As the big forward stood up to play the ball, Malcolm Reilly, who had not been involved in the tackle, nipped in to be marker at the play the ball. This was most unusual so I watched intently to see what happened after the ball had been played. The innocent looking Malcolm flattened Beetson, completely missed by Mr Lancashire, but because Cliff Watson had just tackled Arty, Arty assumed that Cliff was the one who had clouted him! With about 10 minutes to go in the Test match, big Arty threw a punch at Cliff Watson that would have put Cliff in hospital had it connected. Fortunately Cliff ducked. The referee witnessed the whole incident and had no alternative other than to send Beetson off. I looked across at young Malcolm who had a broad grin on his face.

So with a job superbly done, the 1970 British Lions tourists crossed the Tasman Sea to the beautiful, if wet, islands of New Zealand. Seven games had been allocated to this final leg of the tour and the first, only three days after the hard game against Southern New South Wales at

Wollongong, was against a Northern XIII at Tokoroa. The team was Myler; Smith, Hesketh, Hynes, Atkinson; Hardisty, Seabourne; Hartley, Fisher, Watson, Lowe, Thompson and Reilly with Hepworth and Flanagan as subs. Against a keen local side, the tourists ran in seven tries with Syd Hynes crossing for two tries and kicking six goals to give a final score of GB 47 Northern 17.

On 11 July, the New Zealand Kiwis hosted the first Test match of the short tour at Carlaw Park, Auckland. The New Zealand team were Don Ladner [West Coast]; Phil Orchard [Bay of Plenty], Bernie Lowther [Auckland], Roy Christian [Auckland], Mocky Brereton [Canterbury]; Roger Bailey [Auckland], Trevor Patrick [Otago]; Doug Gailey [Auckland], Col O'Neil [Wellington, captain], Robin Orchard [Auckland], John Hibbs [West Coast], Bill Deacon [Waikato] and Tony Kriletich [Auckland]. The Kiwis subs were Fred Shuster [Auckland] and Rod Walker [Canterbury].

Great Britain fielded a strong side, Mick Shoebottom [Leeds], Alan Smith [Leeds], Frank Myler [St Helens, captain], Syd Hynes [Leeds], John Atkinson [Leeds]; Roger Millward [Hull Kingston Rovers], Barry Seabourne [Leeds]; Dennis Hartley [Castleford], Tony Fisher [Bradford Northern], Cliff Watson [St Helens], Doug Laughton [Wigan], Jimmy Thompson [Featherstone Rovers] and Malcolm Reilly [Castleford]. The British subs were Alan Hardisty [Castleford] and Phil Lowe [Hull Kingston Rovers]. The referee was Mr John Percival of Auckland and the attendance was 15,948.

Although the weather was sunny and warm for the game, there had been torrential rain a couple of days before the match and the pitch was ankle deep in mud as play started. The Kiwis were out of their class and only their enthusiasm and fitness plus the expert goal kicking of Don Ladner, with six goals to his credit, kept them in the game. Ladner dropped a goal and kicked a penalty within 15 minutes of the start. Ladner, using the advantage of an 18–7 penalty count, maintained the Kiwis in a position inside the Brits' half. Roger Millward registered one of his tries from the top drawer, Doug Laughton was put over by a superb break and pass from Cliff Watson, Frank Myler and Alan Smith carved up the Kiwi defence for Syd Hynes to dive over. Don Ladner dropped another goal and right on half time, Mick Shoebottom and Mal Reilly combined for John Atkinson to show his pace and score a fine try.

Don Ladner opened the second half with two long range penalty goals and Syd Hynes replied with a neat drop goal. Phil Orchard raised the Kiwis hope with a neat try. Britain went away with a second try by Doug Laughton when he snapped up a Millward kick and plunged over, for Syd Hynes to convert. Don Ladner had the final say with a last minute penalty goal giving the touring Lions a 19–15 win.

It was down the North Island from Auckland to Wellington for the third match against a Wellington XIII and a resounding 60–8 win for Frank's men. The team against Wellington was Dutton; Smith, Shoebottom, Hesketh, Atkinson; Hardisty, Millward; Chisnall, Flanagan, Irving, Lowe, Robinson and Laughton. Alan Smith scored five tries, John Atkinson three, Chris Hesketh two and Doug Laughton, Mick Shoebottom, Peter Flanagan and Phil Lowe one try apiece. Ray Dutton kicked nine goals.

The second Test, played at the Addington Showgrounds in Christchurch on 19 July, meant another flight across the Cook Straight to the South Island of New Zealand. After the closeness of the first Test, it was not surprising that the Kiwis came out fired up. Their enthusiasm, plus some help from the referee, Mr Percival, awarding penalties against the British at the scrums, allowed New Zealand to take a 9–0 lead into the half time dressing room. A Roy Christian try and a conversion plus two towering drop goals from the accurate boot of Don Ladner sent the Kiwis' supporters wild with delight. The New Zealand team was Don Ladner [West Coast]; Phil Orchard [Bay of Plenty], Roy Christian [Auckland], Roger Bailey [Auckland], Mocky Brereton [Canterbury]; Fred Shuster [Auckland], Eric Carson [Auckland]; Doug Gailey [Auckland], Col O'Neil [Wellington captain], Robin Orchard [Auckland], John Hibbs [West Coast], Bill Deacon [Waikato] and Tony Kriletich [Auckland]. Their subs were Wayne Redmond [Auckland] and Kevin Dixon [West Coast].

After the interval Great Britain faced an intense period of early sustained attacks by the Kiwis. This sparked the touring pack to explode suddenly into attacking mode and they began to show their authority in defence too. Frank carved out an opening for Doug Laughton to race through for a try, then Malcolm Reilly and John Atkinson forced their way down field with Frank supporting to take the final pass and romp over. With Ray Dutton converting both tries, Britain had the lead. Roger Millward sliced through for a brace of tries and Malcolm Reilly worked a blind side scrum move with Keith Hepworth which ended with the excellent loose forward dashing over. Ray Dutton finished by scoring four goals making Britain victorious by 23–9.

The Great Britain side for the second Test in Christchurch was, Ray Dutton [Widnes]; Alan Smith [Leeds], Syd Hynes [Leeds], Frank Myler [St Helens], John Atkinson [Leeds]; Roger Millward [Hull Kingston Rovers], Keith Hepworth [Castleford]; Dennis Hartley [Castleford], Tony Fisher [Bradford Northern], Cliff Watson [St Helens], Doug Laughton [Wigan], Jimmy Thompson [Featherstone Rovers] and Malcolm Reilly [Castleford]. The Brits' subs were Mick Shoebottom [Leeds] and Bob Irving [Oldham]. The attendance was 8,600.

The New Zealand Test series now won, Frank and his men were determined to end the tour in style with the magnificent record of losing only one game and drawing one on the whole tour. There were only three games left: West Coast, then back to the North Island for the third Test and finally, the most physical game in New Zealand, the Auckland district team! After the tourists demolished West Coast 57–2, it was back to Auckland for the final two games of the tour.

They played the third Test at Carlaw Park, Auckland on 25 July. This Test turned out to be the toughest game on the New Zealand leg of the tour. Ahead by 11–2 at half time the Kiwis, unfortunately for them, could not last the extremely furious pace set by the British in the second half. The Kiwi side was, Don Ladner [West Coast]; Mocky Brereton [Canterbury], Bernie Lowther [Auckland], Roy Christian [Auckland], Wayne Redmond [Auckland]; Roger Bailey [Auckland], Eric Carson [Auckland], Doug Gailey [Auckland], Col O'Neil [Wellington, captain], Robin Orchard [Auckland], Kevin Dixon [West Coast], Bill Deacon [Waikato] and Tony Kriletich. The two Kiwi subs were Ray Williams [Auckland] and Paul Matete [Auckland].

In the first half the only try scorer for New Zealand was Roger

Bailey. Don Ladner converted the try and kicked two penalty goals and a drop goal. Roger Millward dropped a goal for Britain. In the second half the Kiwis considered that a 'roughing up' style of play would see them home on the back of their half time lead but this only stiffened the resolve of the British pack. Phil Lowe scored two tries and Cliff Watson also recorded a try. Other try scorers for Britain were Alan Smith, Chris Hesketh, Keith Hepworth and Britain's sub back on the day, Syd Hynes. Ray Dutton added five goals to give Great Britain the victory 33–16. The Great Britain side on duty was Ray Dutton [Widnes]; Alan Smith [Leeds], Chris Hesketh [Salford], Frank Myler [St Helens, captain], John Atkinson [Leeds]; Roger Millward [Hull Kingston Rovers], Keith Hepworth [Castleford]; Cliff Watson [St Helens], Tony Fisher [Bradford Northern], Johnny Ward [Salford], Bob Irving [Oldham], Phil Lowe [Hull Kingston Rovers] and Malcolm Reilly [Castleford]. The subs were Syd Hynes [Leeds] and Doug Laughton [Wigan]. Mr Percival was the referee once again and the attendance was 13,137.

The final game of this, the 1970 tour was the traditional one against Auckland at Carlaw Park. The side elected was strong enough to win 23–8 and was Dutton; Irving, Hynes, Hardisty, Atkinson; Millward, Seabourne; Hartley, Flanagan, Chisnall, Thompson, Laughton and Reilly.

Frank's feelings concerning this particular tour were that:

... we became the 10th touring team to win the series in Australia. We travelled to New Zealand on the crest of a wave of confidence and won all our seven games there. It would be silly to attempt to compare players and sides from different eras but if ever there was a better touring side than the one I had the honour and pleasure of captaining on that 1970 tour, they must have been good! The honour was that which I always felt when representing my country, the pleasure was being in the company of so many top class men who toed the line in every aspect of the tour. They were a great bunch of lads. This time I returned to England a very happy man, never dreaming that Australia had not finished with me yet!

14

RETURN TO SAINTS, THE WORLD CUP 1970 AND ROCHDALE

Back at home, both Frank and Cliff Watson were fit and ready to play in the opening game of the season, the Champions v Cup Winners charity game against Castleford on 15 August. In an open football game the result was a 19 all draw.

Frank was at stand off half in 17 of St Helens first 24 games and the season had a successful start. The first league reverse was the 22–8 defeat at Station Road, Swinton only two days after Swinton had been beaten 20–7 at Knowsley Road in the Lancashire Cup. The County Cup began with a 30–3 win away to Huyton, followed by the Swinton victory. Three competitions were taking place simultaneously, the League programme, the Lancashire Cup and the BBC2 Floodlit Trophy. The County Cup and the BBC2 Floodlit Trophy culminated when Saints reached the final in both competitions. The league games continued to run successfully with only the second defeat in the 16th league game of the season to date coming at the hands of Leigh at Hilton Park by 15–13. In the Lancashire Cup Saints were already in the semi final, due to play their old enemy Wigan at Central Park. An outstanding 23–0 win put them into the final at Station Road, Swinton. But the County Cup final was put on ice, along with the BBC2 Floodlit Trophy, until after the World Cup. Great Britain's first game was against the Australians at Headingley on 24 October.

Frank's success as Great Britain captain on the recent tour impressed the selectors who had invited Frank to captain the World

Cup side. Britain's squad of World Cup players was Ray Dutton [Widnes], Paul Charlton [Salford], Alan Smith [Leeds], John Atkinson [Leeds], Keri Jones [Wigan], Mick Shoebottom [Leeds], Syd Hynes [Leeds], Chris Hesketh [Salford], Frank Myler [St Helens, captain], Keith Hepworth [Castleford], Dennis Hartley [Castleford], Cliff Watson [St Helens], Tony Fisher [Bradford Northern], Kevin Ashcroft [Leigh], Dave Chisnall [Leigh], Bob Haigh [Leeds], Jimmy Thompson [Featherstone Rovers], Doug Laughton [Wigan] and Malcolm Reilly [Castleford].

The Great Britain side selected for the first game was Dutton, Smith, Hynes, Myler, Atkinson, Shoebottom, Hepworth, Hartley, Fisher, Watson, Thompson, Laughton and Reilly. The subs were Hesketh and Haigh. The Aussies had made several changes since relinquishing the ashes and fielded a side containing players the British public had not seen before. Their team was Eric Simms [South Sydney]; Lionel Williamson [Newtown], Ray Branighan [South Sydney], Bobby Fulton [Manly], Mark Harris [Eastern Suburbs]; Dennis Pittard [South Dyne], Billy Smith [St George, captain]; John O'Neill [South Sydney], Elwyn Walters [South Sydney], Bob O'Reilly [Parramatta], Bob McCarthy [South Sydney], Paul Sait [South Sydney] and Gary Sullivan [Newtown]. Their subs were Johnny Brown [Norths, Brisbane] and Ron Turner [Cronulla]. The referee was Mr Fred Lindop of Wakefield, and the attendance was 15,169.

In the first minute the referee cautioned John O'Neill for taking a couple of swings at Dennis Hartley. He went on to be cautioned three times in total and it was obvious that his job was to upset the balance of the British team. John O'Neill was lucky to stay on when he was witnessed kicking Hartley on the head as the British prop was tackled. The report in the *Sunday Express* described the game as 'This dour, fearfully hard World Cup game' and that is what it was! The defences of both sides crushed everything that moved. The magic of Roger Millward was missing as he was sidelined from this World Cup with an injury. Britain missed his eye for an opening and his pace off the mark. The Aussie tackling was unidentifiable compared to the recent Test match series in Australia with three and four big men in at almost every tackle. The way to the try lines was barred but Fulton gave Australia the lead with a neat drop goal. At full back, the Aussies had the big kicking find, Eric Simms the aboriginal South Sydney goal kicker, and he followed Fulton's example with another fine drop goal. Ray Dutton answered with a penalty goal as the game neared half time and the players went in for treatment for their bumps and bruises. At 2–4 to the Aussies it was anyone's game.

The tackling became more ferocious, if possible, in the second half and there were a few stand-and-deliver battles between the backs as well as the forwards. On 54 minutes, Malcolm Reilly performed his party trick. Picking up from dummy half, he blasted away from two big hit tackles and as he was stopped, found Doug Laughton on his shoulder. He carried on for 10 yards before being scythed down but again in true British fashion, he somehow got his pass away to Cliff Watson who found Syd Hynes tearing up beside him. Giving the ball to the centre, he watched Hynes gallop over under the posts for a cracking try, Ray Dutton converting. The normally sure Eric Simms missed four very kickable penalties and was wayward with four drops at goal. But the Aussies' biggest culprit was Bob McCarthy who dropped the ball with the line open to him. Ray Dutton covered himself with glory as he stopped Lionel Williamson and Dennis Pittard within seconds of each other with copybook tackles when a try looked certain. On 75 minutes Syd Hynes dropped a great goal to give Great Britain the perfect start in this World Cup.

Four days later on 28 October at Wheldon Road, Castleford hosted its first ever Great Britain game in a Wednesday evening match in one of the worst torrential rain storms in memory! Conditions were so bad in this World Cup game that neither team scored any tries. The British brought in Keri Jones [Wigan] on the wing for Alan Smith and Kevin Ashcroft [Leigh] at hooker for Tony Fisher. The rest of the side remained the same as it had in the first game against the Aussies. Their opponents, France, went for Jean Pierre Cros [Albi]; Serge Marsolan [St Gaudens], Michel Molinier [St Gaudens], Andre Ruiz [Carcassonne], Etienne Bonal [Carcassonne]; Jean Capdouze [Perpignan], Germaine Guiraud [Carcassonne]; Christian Sabatie

[Villeneuve], Jacques Cabero [Perpignan], Ferdy De Nadai [Limoux], Herve Mazard [Lezignan], Gerard Cremoux [Villeneuve] and Jean Pierre Clar [Villeneuve] with Delair Pellerin [Villneneuve] and Francoise Bonet [Albi]. The referee was Mr Fred Lindop of Wakefield and 8,958 brave souls turned out in that monsoon to watch it.

Thanks to Kevin Ashcroft's dominance in the scrums, 17 to 8 and 24 penalties out of 34 to Britain, play was kept well inside the French half for the majority of the game. Jean Capdouze's kicking caused a few problems for Great Britain. In the respect of fielding awkward loose balls in these abysmal conditions, Ray Dutton was magnificent. His three goals were the difference between the two sides. In a forward dominated battle, with mud over the boot tops, Hartley, Watson, Ashcroft and Reilly were outstanding, whilst France's top players were Clar and Mazard.

In the Great Britain v New Zealand game played at Station Road, Swinton on 31 October, Frank withdrew owing to a slight knee problem. Chris Hesketh took his place in the centre and Britain had a comfortable 27–17 win. In times gone by, Great Britain would have been declared winners of the World Cup because of finishing at the top of the league but the laws changed and Great Britain had to play off for the cup against the second place team, Australia. The World Cup final was played at Headingley on 7 November. It might well have been played on 5 November to coincide with all the fireworks going on in this most brutal of games. The weather was perfect, a beautiful autumn afternoon. But the game was not a beautiful sight! The totally disciplined, smoothly drilled play of the recent tour disappeared as players carried on a man on man vendetta. Old scores were settled and many new scores were opened in this result which left the British public dumbfounded!

Australia won the World Cup at Headingley with an overwhelming display of defensive determination and a pack that stood up to a vicious onslaught of punches, kicks, knees, elbows and every kind of brutality. Great Britain were not on their own amongst all this brutality as the Australians were just as guilty. One confrontation between Tony Fisher and big John O'Neill, after Bobby Fulton was left prostrate in an Aussie passing move, saw Fisher being stalked from behind by O'Neill and the whole crowd shouting a warning to the British hooker! Just in time Fisher turned to face the huge Aussie prop and using his experience as a boxing champion in the armed forces, cut both the big man's eyes with the perfect left-right combination! Obviously in trouble, O'Neill called off the contest. The respected writer of the *Daily Mirror*, Joe Humphreys, was amongst the many writers who condemned both sides for the viciousness of the approach to this game. Joe Humphreys wrote of the Great Britain team, 'Though they won the fight, they lost the World Cup, their tempers and their reputations'. Ray Dutton gave Britain the lead with a penalty goal. Australia levelled the score with an Eric Simms penalty and nearing half time Malcolm Reilly was double tackled and lost the ball. Australia regained possession and moved the ball out to the Rev. John Cootes who blasted through a two man tackle to dive over for an unconverted try. On the stroke of half time Syd Hynes dropped a surprise goal directly from acting half back to send Great Britain into the dressing rooms one point behind at 5–4.

The battle commenced again after half time and although this was a crucial Test match and World Cup final, the leniency of Mr Lindop was amazing! Players battered each other both fairly and unfairly, some toe to toe, others facing two or even three opponents. There were burst noses, cut eyes, split lips and every other kind of facial injury on display. Australia scored the crucial try in that second half when Bob McCarthy slipped a neat pass to Lionel Williamson who set sail for the corner. John Atkinson and Mick Shoebottom seemed to have him covered but unfortunately the Leeds pair collided and this gave Williamson the space to slide in at the corner flag, Simms regained his reputation by kicking a monster conversion. Simms added to this kick by dropping a close in goal and it was left to Atkinson to finish off good work by Shoebottom, Hynes and Frank Myler with an unconverted try in the corner. One of the last actions in playing time saw a stand up fight between Syd Hynes and Billy Smith. When the dust settled, referee Lindop had no option but to send off the pair although considering what had gone on prior to their set to, both Smith and Hynes could class themselves as being unlucky. The final whistle sounded with the score Australia 12 Great Britain 7. Immediately came the definite last action as players set about each other again and a huge brawl erupted in the centre of the field. It was a sad end to a World Cup that had seemed to be there for Britain's taking. The discipline that was such a feature of Britain's 1970 tour and the early games of this competition was sadly missing from this final.

November 1970 was a big month in Frank Myler's career. On 7 November, the World Cup Final was his last international game for Great Britain. On 9 November Frank played at stand off for St Helens against the victorious Aussie world champions at Knowsley Road, on 11 November Frank captained the Lancashire County team in his final appearance in inter-county football against Cumberland at Barrow and on 28 November he played at stand off for Saints in the Lancashire Cup Final. Some month!

The Saints team playing against the Aussies were Frank Barrow; Brian Glover, Billy Benyon, John Walsh, Frank Wilson, Frank Myler, Alan Whittle, Graham Rees, Tony Karalius, Cliff Watson, Eric Chisnall, Eric Prescott and Kel Coslett. The subs were Jeff Heaton and Bill Sheffield. In a glorious display of fast, open rugby Saints destroyed Australia 37–10. The feature of the scoring was that all the Saints' tries came from their backs, Whittle (3), Benyon (2), Wilson and Glover (1 each). Kel Coslett kicked six goals and John Walsh kicked two. The victory felt like revenge for both Frank and Cliff Watson.

Frank's final county game was as captain of Lancashire against Cumberland. The Red Rose team was John Walsh [St Helens]; Stuart Wright [Wigan], Billy Benyon [St Helens], Chris Hesketh [Salford], Joe Walsh [Leigh]; Frank Myler [St Helens], Joe Boylan [Widnes]; Dave Chisnall [Leigh], Kevin Ashcroft [Leigh], Eddie Brown [Rochdale Hornets], Eric Chisnall [St Helens], Eric Prescott [St Helens] and Doug Laughton [Wigan]. The subs were Martin Murphy [Oldham] and George Nicholls [Widnes]. The Cumberland side was, Paul Charlton [Salford]; Keith Davies [Workington Town], Ian Wright [Workington Town], Tony Colloby [Salford], Rod Morns [Whitehaven]; Bob Nicholson [Workington Town], Joe Bonner [Wakefield Trinity];

Les Moore [Workington Town], Howard Allen [Workington Town], Frank Foster [Barrow], Harold McCourt [Workington Town], Eddie Bowman [Workington Town] and John 'Spanky' McFarlane [Barrow]. Their one sub was Dennis Martin [Whitehaven]. The referee was Mr Ronnie Jackson of Halifax and the attendance at Craven Park, Barrow was 2,878.

The result was a clear cut 28–5 victory for Lancashire with Frank Myler leading the way with two tries. Others who crossed for them were Stuart Wright, Chris Hesketh, Kevin Ashcroft and Eric Prescott. John Walsh kicked five goals. For Cumberland, Dennis Martin scored a try, and Tony Colloby landed a goal. Being given the responsibility to represent Lancashire had been an important feature of Frank's long and highly successful career. He had enjoyed inter-county rugby and in Frank's day selection for the county was, as mentioned earlier, a stepping stone to full international honours. Again he loved every second of his dual representative selections. He also loved the adrenaline rush of big games in the various cups that were abundant in his playing career.

Because of the World Cup, the final of the Lancashire Cup was postponed until the world championship competition was over. St Helens and Leigh had fought their way through to the final, played at Station Road, Swinton. The semi finals were way back on 10 October. Now it was 28 November and the weather was as could be expected in late November, cold and wet. Leigh were going great guns, approaching a successful period in their club's history under the leadership of Alex Murphy. They had beaten Widnes at Naughton Park in this competition's semi final and went into this game on a fantastic run of 11 wins. But Saints were also having a great run in the league and their magnificent victory over the Aussies sent them into the final winning 11 of their last 12 games. The final had the makings of a great game. But, like most things, this wonderful game did not materialise as the heavy conditions deteriorated with a torrential downpour just before the kick off. The referee was the great Mr Billy Thompson of Huddersfield in front of a crowd of almost 11,000 who witnessed the kick off. The teams were Saints, Frank Barrow; Les Jones, Billy

Benyon, John Walsh, Frank Wilson; Frank Myler, Alan Whittle; Albert Halsall, Tony Karalius, Graham Rees, John Mantle, Eric Chisnall and Kel Coslett [captain]. Their sub was Eric Prescott. Leigh were happy to declare all present and on duty with the following side, Stuart Ferguson; Rod Tickle, Mick Collins, Les Chisnall, Joe Walsh: David Eckersley, Alex Murphy [captain]; Dave Chisnall, Kevin Ashcroft, Derek Watts, Paul Grimes, Geoff Clarkson and Mick Mooney. Their sub was Tommy Canning.

Instead of the expected exciting final, the crowd witnessed a scrappy, bad tempered game where Mr Thompson sent off three men. The dismissed players were the brothers, Les and Dave Chisnall of Leigh and Alan Whittle of Saints. Three Chisnall brothers played in the game, Les and Dave, as already mentioned and Eric of St Helens. Kel Coslett gave Saints the lead with a penalty goal and Stuart Ferguson drew level for Leigh with a fine penalty goal.

Then Coslett again gave Saints the lead with his second goal. The game needed a touch of something inspirational and it came from Alex Murphy when in the dying minutes he put up a devastating spiral punt which had poor Frank Barrow turning that way and this way as he attempted a very difficult overhead catch. Frank Barrow could only watch in dismay as the ball bounced off his shoulder into the air to bounce again off its point, as only a rugby ball can, back into the Saints in goal area to land in front of Dave Eckersley. Eckersley touched down for the winning try and Ferguson added the extra two points. Leigh lifted the old cup with a score of 7–4.

Frank played his final game for St Helens on 13 March 1971 in the win away at Craven Park against Hull Kingston Rovers. Saints won 26–9. Not long after, Rochdale Hornets contacted St Helens to enquire about the availability of Frank and to ask if he would be interested in joining them at the Athletic Grounds as player-coach at the club. As there were only 12 games remaining in the season and Frank had taken a bruise or two in recent games, he asked if Hornets would give him some time to think it over. He was now 32 years old but still fit. His rugby league career had glittered and he had enjoyed every moment but playing at the sharp end without a break since age 17 had been a long haul! He also had the added demands that business placed on him. He was the joint owner of two betting shops and his absences for Saturday matches meant that his partner was often left to cope with the pressures of busy weekend business. After a couple of months of deliberating, and making alternative arrangements with his business partner, Frank decided to take up Rochdale's offer. The saying in the game used to be that as a player-coach if things were not going right on the field, then you could do something about it, as it were, from the front line. As a coach, you sat on your bottom on the bench in the dugout. It was oh so much more difficult to have a big input on a game once your charges had left you and gone out onto the field. But, what the heck, the time was right, and that was what it took to stay in the game he loved. Frank never intended to move from player to coach; as with most things, it just happened.

Whilst obviously looking forward to the new challenge, Frank was sad to leave St Helens where he had spent almost four seasons. He says, 'I thoroughly enjoyed every moment at St Helens. From the minute I arrived both the players and fans made me feel at home and they continued to do so for the length of my stay. The coach and staff were enormously helpful to me and I also had the pleasure and benefit of playing with brilliant players such as Cliff Watson, Kel Coslett, Austin Rhodes, Tommy Bishop, Tom van Vollenhoven, John Walsh, Billy Benyon, Frankie Barrow, Jeff Heaton, Alan Whittle, Frank Wilson, Dave Chisnall and John Warlow to mention just a few. My one disappointment was that when I arrived at St Helens, Alex Murphy, who I considered to be the best number 7 ever, had moved on to join Leigh.'

Frank moved to the Athletic Grounds and started the 1971–72 season. He says:

Rochdale was a great club to be involved with. The Club Secretary Fred Kershaw, Chairman Alan Ellis and Jack Grindrod, who signed me, were great characters. These men were the reason I was at the club. They all had a great sense of humour and the atmosphere within the club from directors, players and fans, was really terrific! In fact, to this day I still like to visit Rochdale to keep in touch with old friends.

When I arrived for the first training session, I knew quite a few of the players and there was a good turnout. The main aim was to get everyone fit for the coming season. However, I also realised that the forwards lacked size and the backs lacked pace so, although there were good players there, we would have to look around the league for some more players.

Rochdale directors had given me a budget but, unfortunately, the money available was not sufficient to buy the best players. However I had a few players in mind who, like me, were approaching the end of their careers. These players were skilled, experienced and would be affordable. My first signing was a great friend of mine, Bill Holliday, who I had played with on the Great Britain side. Bill was a big strong second row forward whose career had started with Whitehaven. I had no doubts about Bill's ability and he was to be our captain. We acquired him from Swinton for the princely sum of £1,000. My next signing was Peter Gartland who had played for St Helens at scrum half in the 'A' team. I remember watching Peter quite often and thought that such a good player shouldn't be playing 'A' team football. After Peter, I signed Willie Aspinall from Warrington at stand off or centre, also Brian Glover from St Helens. Both these players were ex-internationals. Other signings followed, including Tom Brophy from Barrow. Tom had played rugby union for England and was also a neighbour of mine from our schooldays in Widnes.

Frank's season started with a fine away win in the Lancashire Cup at Barrow. His charges on his first outing as coach were Joe Chamberlain; Mike Ratu, Jim Crellin, Albert Hillman, Norman Brelsford; Frank Myler, Trevor Rabbitt; Peter Birchall, Peter Clarke, Eddie Brown, Bob Welding, Bill Sheffield and Henry Delooze. The subs were Peter Gartland and George Snape. In round two a week later, the Hornets were defeated 17–8 by a strong Widnes outfit at Naughton Park, Frank scoring a try against his old club. The league season started brightly enough with home wins against Dewsbury, revenge against Widnes and a fine win at Clarence Street against York. The only blot on the first four league games was a 15–5 defeat at Wheldon Road, Castleford.

Frank's seventh game as player-coach was against the touring Kiwis. This was the New Zealanders' first game of the tour and they selected a strong side for this fixture. Roy Christian, a player Frank had faced on quite a few occasions, captained the Kiwis. Rochdale's team for this game was Joe Chamberlain, Mike Ratu, Jim Crellin, Bob Machen, Norman Brelsford; Frank Myler, Peter Gartland; Peter Birchall, Peter Clarke, Mike Watson, Kevin Flanagan, Bob Welding and Henry Delooze. The subs were Willie Aspinall and Eddie Brown. The New Zealanders' almost Test strength side proved just too good for the Hornets and beat the home outfit 23–8. Jim Crellin and Kevin Flanagan scored tries and Joe Chamberlain landed one goal.

Under Frank's guidance Rochdale did extremely well in the season's BBC2 Floodlit Trophy. The first round was a two legged affair against 'derby' opposition in Oldham. In the first leg, the Hornets were at home and won 28–2. Oldham won the second leg at The Watersheddings 16–14, sending the Hornets into the second round by an aggregate score of 42–18. Salford, at the Willows, were beaten next by 17–15. The third round brought Widnes to the Athletic Grounds and another great 6–5 win took Rochdale into the semi final with a home draw against Hull FC. A cracking win against Hull FC by 30–8 was followed by the final of the BBC2 Floodlit Trophy. This was a tough game against St Helens at Knowsley Road.

In the final Rochdale Hornets' team consisted of Chamberlain; Brelsford, Crellin, David Taylor, Brian Glover; Frank Myler, Gartland; Birchall, Clarke, Brown, Welding, Sheffield and Delooze. Their subs were John Hammond and Alan Hodkinson. St Helens fielded Geoff Pimblett; Les Jones, Billy Benyon, John Walsh, Frank Wilson; Ken Kelly, Jeff Heaton, Graham Rees, Tony Karalius, Eric Chisnall, Eric Prescott, John Mantle and Kel Coslett. The Saints' subs were John Houghton and John Stephens. Heavy rain and deep mud greeted the players as they trudged onto the St Helens pitch. After all the preliminaries the game began, but the weather and some real hard defences stopped any sort of open play, as the forwards ground out a tight and hard fought game. The Saints' ace was goal kicker Kel Coslett who landed four goals to Joe Chamberlain's one in an 8–2 win for St Helens. A crowd of 9,300 witnessed the game and applauded the efforts of the players who produced a good game to watch in terms of wholehearted endeavour.

Frank was pleased with this effort, and had praise for his pack in the local newspaper. In those days the season was a long hard grind and Rochdale played 48 games that season. Playing 30 times at stand off half, two games in the centre, plus one substitute appearance made Frank a good signing for the Hornets that season. His 33 games were good for a strong running middle back. Joe Chamberlain at full back and Norman Brelsford on the wing played in all 48 games but they were slightly isolated from the workload of players such as hooker Peter Clarke who missed only four games in the whole season. When you stop to consider the position of hooker in the days of competitive scrums and think of the number of tackles expected from any hooker in midfield, his 44 appearances that season verged on the miraculous!

Rochdale disappeared early from both the John Player Trophy and Challenge Cup competitions. A 12–8 win in the John Player against Bradford Northern at Odsal in round one was cancelled out in the following round in a 14–4 defeat at the hands of Blackpool at the Athletic Grounds. The Challenge Cup saw the Hornets travel to Clarence Street, York where the home side ground out a hard fought 12–5 win. The 'derby' games with Oldham went two apiece in the four games played and although the BBC2 Floodlit Trophy Final was the crowning glory of the season, Rochdale played brilliantly to reach the championship play off. Rochdale beat Wakefield Trinity at home 18–13 and in the second round of the championship, the Hornets had to travel to play St Helens. In the final game of Frank's first season his side were beaten by an honourable 17–5. The teams on the day were Saints, Geoff Pimblett; John Wills, John Houghton, John Walsh, Frank Taylor; Alan Whittle, Jeff Heaton; John Stephens, Tony Karalius, Graham Rees, Eric Prescott, John Mantle and Kel Coslett, with their subs, Alan

Gwilliam and Kelvin Earl. The Hornets, without their injured player-coach fielded, Joe Chamberlain; Norman Brelsford, Jim Crellin, John Hammond, Tommy Pimblett; Willie Aspinall, Peter Gartland; Peter Birchall, Terry O'Neill, Alan Hodkinson, Bob Welding, Kevin Flanagan and Henry Delooze. Subs for the Hornets were Mick Crocker and Eddie Brown. Looking back on his first dabble in coaching, Frank could have been well pleased with the effort his players put in and the progress the club made in the season.

15

PLAYING ENDS AND COACHING BEGINS

Frank was in business for himself as a painter and decorator and he also had a couple of bookies shops in Widnes. The bumps and bruises he attracted at almost 34 years of age were hurting a lot more than when he was a 24 year old! He had always played a style of rugby league which thought little of those bumps and bruises as he was making a break or a tackle. Now they were taking longer to recover from. Nevertheless, Frank started pre-season training, and his players were in confident mood as the 1972–73 season approached. Saints were their first opponents of the season and the visitors won 21–3. Barrow's former England rugby union star back, Tom Brophy, had moved to Rochdale on transfer during the closed season and showed his worth as a goal kicker in the second game of the season in the 11–10 win away at Castleford, Brophy landing four goals. Frank made a start to the season in the Lancashire Cup first round 24–19 win up at Whitehaven, and scored a try in that game to go with the five tries from Norman Brelsford. After the Saints defeat in the first game Frank recorded four consecutive wins against Castleford, Workington Town at home 14–10, the win in the County Cup and a great 8–4 win away to Hull Kingston Rovers.

Frank still had something left in the tank that season as in 16 starts and one substitution he scored eight tries and made many more. But the time came when Frank decided to call it a day as a player. That day was 7 January 1973 and his opponents were Salford at the Athletic Grounds. The result, unfortunately, was a 13–11 win for Salford. In the last game Frank played as part of Rochdale Hornets, the team was made up of Willie Aspinall; Norman Brelsford, Tom Brophy, David Taylor, Albert

Hillman; Frank Myler, Peter Gartland; Bill Holliday, Ray Harris, Stuart Whitehead, Kevin Flanagan, Bill Sheffield and Alan Robinson.

It had been a wonderful medal-winning career and Frank had some terrific memories of his time playing the game. He had played with, and against, the best players in the world and was held in the greatest respect throughout the rugby league playing nations. Some of the highlights of the 1972–73 season include the league double over Hull Kingston Rovers, a 22–8 win over Wigan at home, a League double over old enemies Oldham and Barrow and a seven points all draw at home to Leigh. There was also a cracking 12–5 win away against Leigh (who took some beating just then) and a championship play off 14–10 win against Salford at the Willows. Frank continued as coach until October 1974 taking Rochdale to the John Player Trophy final, but losing 16–27 to Warrington at Wigan on 9 February 1974. Now he was leaving to look to his business and at the time he didn't consider coaching or any other job in the game's management. But rugby league is inclined to sneak up on you without you knowing and when one has had so much to do with the game it is very hard indeed to shut it out completely.

Frank remembers:

I had played the last game of my international career in the 1970 World Cup where we beat the Australians in the first round but lost to them in the final. Just over two years later I retired from playing at the age of 35. At that time I had no thought of becoming either a manager or coach, all I wanted to do was concentrate on my business interests. I had enjoyed my spell at Rochdale immensely and the string to my bow as player-coach was fine but the part of coaching where I had to sit helpless on the bench unable to do anything if the lads were playing poorly was frustrating. I had no thought of becoming a manager or coach for any team and after 19 years in the game, I thought I'd had enough.

But when you had been at the sharp end of the game as long as I had and you live amongst people, as I do, who regard watching rugby league as their principal recreation, I was forced to reconsider. Another thing I couldn't escape, which retained my interest in the game, was the rugby league talk in pubs and clubs.

Then finally in 1975 I was tempted back by the invisible strands that tie players to their former clubs, especially as the club was my first professional club and my home town outfit, Widnes. I took on the managerial responsibility and spent three years there. In the role of manager-coach I took the club to back-to-back Wembley Challenge Cup finals in 1976 (in a 20–5 loss to St Helens) and in 1977 (in another loss, 16–7, against Leeds). In 1978 business commitments once again encroached upon my rugby career. I discussed my situation with the Widnes committee and advised them that I had decided to call it a day. During my time at Widnes, the club won the Lancashire Cup in 1975 and 1976, the John Player Trophy 1975–76 and were also finalists at Wembley in 1976 and 1977. In the 1977–78 season Widnes won their first First Division Championship and in the same year I received the Man of Steel Coach of the Year award.

At Widnes Frank was surrounded by some great characters, not least of these was Big Jim Mills. The memory of one or two incidents involving Jim still brings a smile to his face. On one occasion Jim had just returned after a four match suspension. Frank recalls the details:

Widnes were playing Wigan who were being coached at that time by Vince Karalius. Prior to the kick off I made a comment to Jim that after having just come back he should be careful not to be too aggressive. I told him that, knowing Vin, he would obviously have one of his players ready to wind him up! Within the first 10 minutes of the game, Bill Ashurst the Wigan loose forward, ran towards Jim and, as Jim was about to tackle him around the shoulders, Ashurst stuck his elbow out and caught Jim in the Adam's apple. Within seconds the Wigan player had received three punches before hitting the deck. The result was that Jim was sent off and the Wigan player retired to the dressing room. You can imagine how upset I was having particularly warned Jim of this possibility. At half time I made sure I was first into the dressing room to have a quick word with him. As I walked in to give him a dressing down, Jim was in the bath, his face like thunder. He just looked at me and said, 'Don't open your mouth Frank!'

Obviously he was in no mood for a dressing down so I just said, 'I've only come in to say that was a great left hook!' and quickly retreated.

On another occasion, during a team talk, we were discussing stats of previous matches relating to the number of tackles a player had made during a game. Jim was at the bottom of the list having made just one tackle. I told him he had the lowest count and asked him why this was. During this time Jim had been seated, but before he answered my question he stood up and stretched to his full 6 feet 5 inches and said, 'If you were a player Frank I'm sure you'd sooner run at somebody else rather than me.' Everyone burst out laughing and that was the end of the conversation about tackling tactics.

Despite the many humorous incidents involving Jim off the field, on the field he was deadly serious. For such a big man he was quite nimble on his feet. He certainly played a big part in the success of Widnes. He scored many tries from 30 yards out. Once he was in full pace he was hard to bring down. In the days when the ball had to be put into the scrum properly at number 8 he excelled, along with Keith Elwell, in getting possession from the scrum.

Midway through my stay at Widnes, Jim asked for a transfer due to an offer he had had from Workington. The club and I didn't want to lose him but I believed if a player wanted to move then we shouldn't stand in his way. As he was adamant he wanted to move I reluctantly agreed to his transfer. However, 12 months later, Jim asked if I was interested in having him back and I welcomed him with open arms.

In 1978, after having some very happy and memorable times at Widnes, Frank decided to call it a day. Doug Laughton, who took over from him, was also a local lad which maintained a degree of consistency in much the same way as when Frank had inherited the team that Vince Karalius had built up. Doug Laughton was a great player in his day and history has proved him to be an exceptional coach who was dedicated to the town and the team. But after 20 months out of the game, Frank was approached by Swinton to take over as team manager in January 1980:

Ex-Swinton player, Peter Smethhurst, joined me as assistant coach. I told them I would give it my best shot for 12 months and then see how things went. I knew it would be a hard job but I wouldn't have taken it on if I hadn't thought Swinton could improve. I knew there was little chance of promotion that season but I was aiming to get within striking distance.

Prior to the start of the 1980–81 season, in an attempt to build on youth, I signed Paul Mellor, a promising 17 year old from the Langworthy club. Dennis Ashcroft from Oldham was also signed and we decided to put some other players on the transfer list. Other additions to the team were Green Vigo, the South African we signed from Wigan, and the Maori stand off, Wayne Rutene, who arrived on a short term contract. Earlier I had brought in Alan Taylor, a half back, from Widnes and we had signed a 24 year old stand off, Danny Wilson, from Wales. Danny had previously played rugby union with Cardiff, Newport and Butetown Rugby Union clubs. On signing for Swinton he moved his wife and two young sons, three year old Rhodri and five year old Ryan, up north. Ryan later took his mother's maiden name, Giggs, and found fame in his own right on the football pitch.

The team soon had a solid and settled look about it with John Gorton, a reliable goal kicking full back, and the three quarter line of Green Vigo, Danny Wilson, Alva Drummond and either Gordon Graham or Bob Bruen. Then there was the experience at half back in the form of Rutene and captain Alan Taylor, whilst Johnny Mellor remained an outstanding prospect. The established prop forwards were Dennis Ashcroft and Alan Grice with Alan Derbyshire at hooker. The back row varied between Dave Nicholson, Tommy Highton and Tony Cooper. Kevin O'Loughlin covered a variety of positions and Tony Peters made the number 13 shirt his own.

Behind the scenes, away from the playing pitch, there were major financial problems brewing. Whilst there were improvements being made on the pitch, off it the club was in serious financial difficulties. Over the 1980–81 season, as a whole, the Swinton Lions had shown a dramatic improvement and the club was in a stronger position, in terms of playing staff, than it had been for many years. However, if Swinton had been promoted they would have had to buy and there was no money available to do so.

During the close season I was approached by Ray Hatton, the Chairman of Oldham, to ask if I would consider taking over as coach at Oldham. At that time, Oldham were in the Second Division but he said that they were going all out to win the Second Division Championship, which would put them into the First Division. He gave me a breakdown of the strength of the team. I knew a few of the players who were already at Oldham, Terry Flanagan, Paddy Kirwin and Ray Ashton, a Widnes lad. They were all young players who I thought could make the grade in the First Division. Ray Hatton told me that there was money available to strengthen the team further.

Leaving Swinton wasn't an easy decision to make. I'd had a good time at the club and the fans were fantastic. However, I had said from the outset that I would give it my best shot and re-evaluate my position after 12 months. So, when the Oldham offer was made I decided the time was right for me to seek a new challenge and I accepted the offer. Peter Smethurst, who was offered the job of assistant coach, joined me in the move to Oldham.

Peter Smethurst and I had a successful first season at Oldham. The club won the Second Division Championship at their first attempt and out of the 32 games played we won 30. As Second Division Champions we won the Slalom Lager Rose Bowl and a prize of £6,000. This was Oldham's first trophy since 1964. Also in that season, Oldham reached the first semi final of a major trophy for 17 years, losing 22–6 to Hull at Headingley in the John Player Trophy.

Having won the Second Division Championship we then had to concentrate on strengthening the side. During the close season we paid a total of £20,000 to Swinton for two players, second row forward Dave Nicholson and scrum half/stand off Alan Taylor. We also bought hooker and good ball player Alan McCurrie from Wakefield at a cost of £35,000 and paid £18,000 to Widnes for prop forward number 8 Brian Hogan. These four players would certainly strengthen the team for the coming season in the First Division.

During the 1982–83 season Oldham finished eighth in the First Division. This was Oldham's best season since 1960–61. We went to table topping Hull in the top eight play off and gave them a mighty fright before losing 24–21. During the season we had acquired Green Vigo from Swinton and Des Foy from Widnes in a deal that saw Hogan go back to Widnes. We also signed Mick Morgan and Wally Jones from Carlisle and Rochdale respectively. Two of our players, Terry Flanagan and Andy Goodway, were selected for the Great Britain team versus France.

Among the people around me at Oldham during that time were Ray Hatton the Chairman, Alan Bonelle the physio, Brian Gartland the Colts coach, Peter Smethurst the assistant coach, John Watkins the sponge man, Donald Walton the club doctor and Terry Flanagan the club captain. The squad was largely composed of Gordon Pollard, Les Cook, Geoff Munro, Phil Ward, Brian Hogan, Andy Goodway, Clive Hunter, Mick Worrall, Ashley McEwen, Gareth Owen, Martin Murphy, Dave Nicholson, Paul Lowndes, Dennis O'Neill, Mick Parrish, Brian Caffery, Alan Taylor, Bob Mordell, Alan McCurrie, Ray Ashton and Paddy Kirwan.

Halfway through the 1982–83 season, Peter Smethurst went to Leigh as first team coach. He was replaced by Frankie Barrow. Before the end of the season I left temporarily to take over as full time GB coach for the 1984 tour and Peter came back from Leigh to assume control with Frankie as his number 2. However things didn't work out for either of them and they both resigned leaving Brian Gartland to see out the season as temporary boss. Despite all these problems the side managed to finish 10th out of 16 in the First Division.

Away from Oldham, in his role as GB coach, Frank selected Ashton, Foy,

Worrall and Goodway for the tour, and when Chris Arkwright of St Helens failed a fitness test, he brought in Terry Flanagan. This gave Oldham a record five players on tour:

I honestly believe that once you have been involved in a Lions tour of Australia and New Zealand you somehow become involved in the history of all previous Lions tours. Some tours have been raging successes whilst others have not been so successful. The 1974 tour was heroic but unfortunately the Lions lost the Aussie Test series 2 to 1 but won the Kiwi series by the same margin. One can tell from the score in the final Test how close the 1974 tourists came to winning the ashes, 22–18! We went through a similar trauma in 1966.

In March 1983 I was asked to take over the job of coach for this tour. I didn't hesitate for one moment. I regarded this appointment as an honour and a great responsibility. I was always proud to represent my country and this offer was too much for me to refuse although I knew it would be a long, hard road. Victory in a Test match requires hard training, dedication and great players. I could do my bit in several directions but I couldn't make great players. I knew Australia had a few great players but I had to hope that I could find some to match them in our leagues.

The first job for the team manager and me was to pencil in the nucleus of players with experience of playing in Australia. As we could take the new number of players on tour, 30 instead of the traditional 26, we decided that we should pick around seven or eight experienced men. After discussions we agreed on 10 players who had toured in 1979. We invited these 10 players into the training squad. They were Mick Adams [Widnes], Steve Evans [Featherstone Rovers], George Fairbairn [Hull Kingston Rovers], Phil Hogan [Hull Kingston Rovers], John Joyner [Castleford], Keith Mumby [Bradford Northern], Trevor Skerrett [Hull FC], Dave Topliss [Wakefield Trinity], John Woods [Leigh] and Dave Watkinson [Hull Kingston Rovers]. I added Len Casey [Hull Kingston Rovers] to the squad a little later. Early on, I selected

Trevor Skerrett as tour captain.

What is that saying about the best laid plans? Only three of these players made the plane. Watkinson broke a leg; Skerrett damaged knee ligaments; Evans and Woods withdrew because of personal reasons; Hogan, Topliss and Fairbairn were injured and the only three who finally made it were Mick Adams, Keith Mumby and John Joyner. Len Casey was banned for six months on the Monday before we flew out! He had been involved in a tussle with a touch judge in a match at Hull Kingston Rovers. When historians look back on our side they will condemn us for taking such an inexperienced squad. Little will they know how we tried!

One thing was in our favour. In September 1983 the Rugby League Rules Committee had brought in the 'six tackle turnover' rule designed to encourage more open play. No longer would the team be able to hang onto the ball for five tackles then boot it into touch. This meant that the number of scrums was drastically reduced, freeing forwards for a more active role in attack. If we could find young players of speed and skill, the type that Britain traditionally produced in greater numbers than Australia, then this new rule might work to our advantage. I knew that my priority was to find such players who could also tackle. After the Test series in 1982 in Britain, it was obvious that we would get nowhere in Test rugby until we had improved this aspect of our game. This new rule would also demand first rate standards of fitness as both forwards and backs would have to do more running and supporting than under the old rule.

Our failure to find sufficient numbers of these type of players was due to a number of factors. In my opinion, the main reason was the gradual decline in the 1970s of the number of school boys playing rugby league in their secondary schools. The basic skills of rugby league need to be learned at an early age. The skills become instinctive in boys who spend most of their spare time with a rugby ball in their hands. Similarly, the tough attitude of mind one needs to play such a physical game is not something easily developed later in life. Today's research finds that an alarming proportion of our youngsters are overweight. This is not surprising for too many children nowadays are content to spend their free time in armchairs watching other people perform when they should be out on a field playing themselves.

We made sure that our players on the 1984 tour would be fit. A specialist physical training guru from Carnegie College in Leeds, Rod McKenzie, was appointed to arrange individual training schedules for all the players, plus regular group sessions as well. We considered players who could not cope with the hard discipline of getting fit for the tour not worthy of selection. We also worked with the squad on tackling and defensive formations. I knew that if we couldn't hit the Aussies hard, we couldn't win! During the 1983–84 season in Great Britain we were due to play the French twice in full international matches and twice at under-24 level. The tour manager, Dick Gemmell and I hoped to use these matches as testing grounds for our ideas on a final touring squad.

The first of these games was a full Test match in Avignon in January 1984, and was a disappointment in many ways. One pleasing aspect was that Great Britain's tackling seemed to have improved and one or two 'finds' emerged amongst those making their first international appearance, notably Keith Rayne the Leeds front rower, who won the man of the match award.

The teams on show that afternoon were Great Britain: Keith Mumby [Bradford Northern captain]; Des Drummond [Leigh], Ronnie Duane [Warrington], Des Foy [Oldham], Garry Clark [Hull Kingston Rovers]; Joe Lydon [Widnes], David Cairns [Barrow]; Keith Rayne [Leeds], David Watkinson [Hull Kingston Rovers], Andy Goodway [Oldham], Mick Worrall [Oldham], David Hobbs [Featherstone Rovers] and David Hall [Hull Kingston Rovers]. The subs were Ellery Hanley [Bradford Northern] and Lee Crooks [Hull FC]. France, stronger than of late, fielded Patrick Wosniak [Villefranche]; Patrick Solal [Hull FC], Didier Bernard [Carcassonne], Philippe Fourquet [Toulouse], Hugues Ratier [Lezignan]; Andre Perez [Toulouse], Christian Scicchitano [Carpentras]; Max Chantel [Villeneuve, captain], Thierry Bernabe [Le Pontet], Pierre Ailleres [Toulouse], Marc Palanque [Carcassonne], Guy Laforgue

[Perpignan] and Dominique Baloup [La Reole]. Their subs were Roger Palisse [St Esteve] and Manuel Caravaca [Limoux]. The referee was Mr John Gocher of Australia and the attendance was 4,200.

There was cruel luck for David Watkinson who broke his leg after only two minutes, Lee Crooks taking his place. Joe Lydon broke a finger and was replaced by the enthusiastic Ellery Hanley. Lee Crooks landed a 60th penalty goal after a point-less first half, so strong had the defences been in the first 40 minutes. Andy Goodway charged a kick down, and recovered the ball to race 40 yards to score a try. This was the first four point try recorded by a British player in a Test match. Late in the game Keith Rayne broke superbly to race clear and send Des Foy tearing over for Lee Crooks to convert. Frank remembers the second Test match against France:

The second French Test was due to be played at Headingley in the following month, February. We were still looking for players with commitment and skill and there were always plenty of players waiting for the opportunity to force their way into contention for a place on the tour. Unfortunately, some club coaches were reluctant to release their players for training sessions, because training sessions were on mid week evenings and they interfered with normal club training. Obviously, on the weekends that club matches were played it was difficult, as in those days players were also in full time employment and rugby was secondary. Nevertheless, I had to stand by my public statement that players who did not train with the squad would not be considered for selection for international matches. Subsequently the team that played against France was, therefore, something of a makeshift one so that the results were not as bad as some critics made out.

The Great Britain team at Headingley was Keith Mumby [Bradford Northern]; Garry Clark [Hull Kingston Rovers], John Joyner [Castleford], Garry Schofield [Hull FC], John Basnett [Widnes]; Ellery Hanley [Bradford Northern], David Cairns [Barrow]; Keith Rayne [Leeds], Brian Noble [Bradford Northern], Kevin Ward [Castleford], Dick Jasiewicz [Bradford Northern], David Hobbs [Featherstone Rovers] and David Hall [Hull

Kingston Rovers]. France made changes at centre, where Palisse came in from sub duty for Bernard who moved onto the wing to replace Ratier. Patrick Trinque [St Esteve] replaced Bernabe at hooker and Jean-Louis Meurin [Albi] came into the second row for Palanque. Mr Gocher was the referee again and the attendance was almost 8,000.

Frank was correct in saying that some critics were harsh on the British performance. The *Yorkshire Post*'s Raymond Fletcher called the 10–0 win by Great Britain, 'an embarrassing victory over France'. David Hobbs kicked five goals as Britain were denied a try in this game. Trevor Watson in the *Yorkshire Evening Post* said the offences by the French 'varied from the daft to downright nasty'. The French side lost discipline and Dominique Baloup pushed Mr Gocher in the back when appealing against a penalty kick and was lucky to get only the yellow card on 47 minutes. After 59 minutes, this incident was followed by Didier Bernard trampling on Brian Noble, after which the Bradford hooker needed five stitches. Another penalty to Britain in the final minutes saw Hobbs kick at goal with the crowd chanting 'boring, boring'. Guy Laforgue was credited with the man of the match.

Frank was philosophical enough to accept that, whilst the match results were not what he had looked for, the French Tests had unearthed two great prospects to rank with the Aussies, Garry Schofield and Ellery Hanley. He continued:

> The squad that Dick Gemmell and I finally selected was, in our minds, the best currently available. We knew that in the vintage touring teams of the past some of our players would not have been considered and I knew in my heart that only about half were good enough to be genuine Test material, but they were all keen to go and they were fit and willing to serve their country.

16

THE 1984 TOUR AND LIFE
AFTER FOOTBALL

The squad for the 1984 tour was Mick Adams [Widnes], Ray Ashton [Oldham], Kevin Beardmore [Castleford], Mick Burke [Widnes], Chris Burton [Hull Kingston Rovers], Brian Case [Wigan], Garry Clark [Hull Kingston Rovers], Lee Crooks [Hull FC], Steve Donlan [Leigh], Des Drummond [Leigh], Ronnie Duane [Warrington], Terry Flanagan [Oldham], Des Foy [Oldham], Andy Goodway [Oldham], Andy Gregory [Widnes], Ellery Hanley [Bradford Northern], David Hobbs [Featherstone Rovers], Neil Holding [St Helens], John Joyner [Castleford], Joe Lydon [Widnes], Keith Mumby [Bradford Northern], Tony Myler [Widnes], Brian Noble [Bradford Northern], Mike O'Neill [Widnes], Harry Pinner [St Helens], Wayne Proctor [Hull FC], Keith Rayne [Leeds], Garry Schofield [Hull FC], Mike Smith [Hull Kingston Rovers] and Mick Worrall [Oldham]. John Basnett [Widnes] replaced the injured Ronnie Duane. The captain was Brian Noble and the physiotherapist was the experienced Ronnie Barritt [Bradford Northern].

Arriving in Australia, the first port of call was, as usual, Darwin. Northern Territory were defeated 40–13 before a decent attendance of 7,216. The bad news in this game was key centre Ronnie Duane's serious knee ligament damage that ended his tour after only 10 minutes' play. Ronnie was a big, fast, rugged centre and was our answer to the size and pace of Gene Miles and Mal Meninga in the forthcoming Tests. The tour management dreads this type of injury, especially when it happens early in the tour. It was closer in the second game of the tour at Wagga Wagga against Riverina where the home district showed determination all through the game, losing to the tourists 22–18. North Coast were taken on in Wauchope, the farming area just inland from Port Macquarie. This was a one sided affair with the tourists romping home by 56–6. The next fixture was out in the bush at Dubbo against Western Division in a real struggle for Frank's men as the locals took the tourists all the way in a 36–30, brawny battle before the Brits held out to win. The victory came at a cost as Tony Myler had to be substituted in the second half. Tony was the first choice stand off for the crucial first Test and had undergone surgery on his knee several months before. He had three thorough medical checkups by specialists who all declared him fit to tour but in this game at Dubbo, the knee swelled and he was in pain. The wisest thing was not to risk him in the crucial first Test. In the first four matches, Britain lost its two most penetrative runners and strongest midfield defenders, but they had to soldier on.

The fifth game of the tour was at the Sydney Cricket Ground against North Sydney Bears. As sometimes happens in times of stress, a youngster grabs the nettle and takes a huge step forward in his career. The lad who did this for Frank was Garry Schofield who was only 18 years old and had a fine game against the Bears, making a try for his wingman and tackling strongly in a 14–8 win. Then it was back up the coast to Newcastle, a traditionally hard place, usually selected to intimidate the tourists immediately before the first Test. It was a hard, verging on brutal, game won by Great Britain, and was much closer than the 28–18 score appears.

Frank recalls:

With Ronnie Duane and Tony Myler missing, our intended three middle backs for the first Test left only John Joyner in place. It seemed inevitable then that sooner or later before the Test match he would break down. That had been our luck since arriving in Australia! Lo and behold, John pulled a hamstring in training and, despite intense physiotherapy, had to be withdrawn from the team. John Joyner had been one of the successes of the 1979 tour and had played in all three Tests. His loss deprived us of the only back we had with experience of playing in a Test match in Australia. Our situation was becoming desperate!

Despite the crippling injuries, the morale and team spirit of our party remained high. Neil Holding the Saints half back is a born entertainer and a brilliant mimic. He kept us entertained throughout the tour. We played tapes on those long coach trips and our theme song was 'High Hopes'. I only know one other song beside this and whilst on holiday in Cork, I won a prize for singing 'High Hopes'. The prize was the title of the second worst singer in Ireland!

Finally we reached the day of the first Test at the Cricket Ground. We decided to play Keith Mumby in the centre because of his strong defensive qualities with his Bradford Northern team mate, Ellery Hanley, on his wing.

The Australian team for the first Test was Garry Jack [Balmain]; Kerry Boustead [Manly], Gene Miles [Wynnum-Manly], Brett Kenny [Parramatta], Ross Conlon [Canterbury-Bankstown]; Wally Lewis [Wynnum-Manly captain], Mark Murry [Redcliffe]; Dave Brown [Manly], Greg Conescu [Gladstone Brothers], Greg Dowling [Wynnum-Manly], Wayne Pearce [Balmain], Brian Niebling [Redcliffe] and Ray Price [Parramatta]. Their subs were Chris Close [Manly] and Chris Young [St George]. Great Britain went into this game unbeaten on tour so far. Their side was Mick Burke [Widnes]; Des Drummond [Leigh], Garry Schofield [Hull FC], Keith Mumby [Bradford Northern], Ellery Hanley [Bradford Northern]; Des Foy [Oldham], Neil Holding [St Helens]; Lee Crooks [Hull FC], Brian Noble [Bradford Northern captain], Andy Goodway [Oldham], Chris Burton [Hull Kingston Rovers], Mick Worrall [Oldham] and Mick Adams [Widnes]. The British subs were Joe Lydon [Widnes] and David Hobbs [Featherstone Rovers]. The referee was Mr R. Shrimpton of New Zealand and the attendance was a startlingly poor 30,190, compared to the first Sydney Test in 1970, when 61,000 attended and in 1974 when 48,000 attended.

In true Test tradition, the first scrum erupted in a huge free for all with Lee Crooks, Andy Goodway and Dave Brown all cautioned. Half way through the first session, Ross Conlon had kicked a penalty goal and Wally Lewis inter passed with Wayne Pearce to race under the posts for the first four points try in an Ashes Test, Ross Conlon converting. Late in the half Mick Burke kicked a penalty goal for Britain to send our boys into the dressing rooms 8–2 behind.

Lee Crooks and Greg Dowling had a set-to which earned them both a yellow card just after Brett Kenny and Wayne Pearce created an opening for Ray Price to crash over for Ross Conlon to convert. Britain hit back with a brilliant try when Des Drummond and Joe Lydon sent young Garry Schofield sprinting in by the posts and Mick Burke converted. Kerry Boustead romped in under the bar for Ross Colon to convert and Wally Lewis dropped a one point goal before Mark Murray charged in directly from a scrum for an unconverted try. Greg Conescu and David Hobbs clashed and Hobbs was sent off by Mr Shrimpton, booed all the way to the dressing room. Conescu was carried off on a stretcher, Australia winning 25–8.

Again Frank recalls:

Of the four half backs we took on this tour only Keith Holding was fit enough to play in this first Test. Des Foy was pressed into marking the great Australian captain, Wally Lewis. Des, a centre, had only limited experience at stand off but he still had more experience than anyone else. Another big blow to us was the late knee injury to one of our toughest forwards, Keith Rayne. Mick Adams became the only player in the team who had ever played in a Test match in Australia. Then Neil Holding had to leave the field with knee ligament problems. He had been worrying the Aussies with his darting runs. With no one in front of him with Test experience, Lewis had a field day. But every player had given his all that day and the Aussies were generous in their praise of our injury ridden team display. Although I have made sweeping statements about the Australians, it is only when playing in Test matches or series that they are the dreaded enemy! Off the field of play there are no finer blokes.

In 1983 I was over there looking for players as the then

Oldham manager. I was invited to the biggest match in their local fixtures, the State of Origin game between New South Wales and Queensland. There I met up with some of my most deadly antagonists in Test football, two in particular, Reg Gasnier and Graeme Langlands.

The Aussies love their rugby league. The Australian fans live and breathe the game. One Sunday morning in 1966 I was out early looking for a Catholic church and I stopped an old chap to ask where the nearest RC church was. He looked at me with a blank expression, then he said, 'Don't ask me mate, I'm RL!' Surely it could only be in Australia that one could find a Catholic priest who was also a Test player. I attended Mass once, and the priest conducting the Mass was Father Coote of Australian international rugby league fame. Most of the congregation were young schoolboys who attended Mass in their clean rugby strips then ran out of church and played their game. There was no disrespect in their actions, as playing rugby was something natural to them and clean rugby kit was perfectly proper wear for going to Mass in.

The second Test was in Brisbane so the team again packed up their belongings to travel once more. Wide Bay District in Bundaberg was the destination and another difficult game ended in a win for the Brits by 28–18. Central Queensland were beaten in sunny Rockhampton by 44–12 then it was up to the beautiful area of Townsville to play North Queensland who were beaten 38–20. It was inland then to the lush farming area of Toowoomba and a shock to the tourists' system. The local boys won 18–16 before the trek across to Brisbane for the second Test.

Frank thinks back:

For this vital second Test, which we had to win to keep the series alive, we were able, at last, to play our first choice stand off, Tony Myler. Although Tony had played only half a game on tour everyone knew he was one of our top class Test players and it was essential that Wally Lewis was contained if we were to have a realistic chance of success. Australia had made changes and selected a trio of huge three quarters with Mal Meninga, and Gene Miles in their centres and Eric Grothe on the wing. This meant that our young backs were now conceding almost two stone per man to their opposite Aussie three quarters. Despite tackling like Trojans, they could not manage on two crucial occasions to hold first Gene Miles then Mal Meninga, and these two breaks led to tries by Eric Grothe and Mal Meninga himself. Loose forward Wayne Pearce had an outstanding game and scored a good try. Mal Meninga kicked three goals to give the Aussies their 18 points. Our six points came from the best try of the game by Garry Schofield and a wonder conversion by Mick Burke. Garry had matured as a player on this tour and his try was a real beauty. But it was all too late; we had failed to regain the ashes.

The game turned very rough towards the end with dangerous high tackles going in from both sides. In their usual fashion the Aussie press blamed it all on the 'vicious Poms', simply ignoring all the facial injuries to the British players such as Brian Noble's broken nose! Some stupid writers were even urging the Aussie players to go out in the final Test and take revenge on certain opponents by attempting to cripple them. Sure, they are only trying to increase their newspaper sales but there are much better ways of doing that than preaching mayhem on the playing field. I would have loved to see some of these reporters out there on the pitch trying to put into practice what they were telling their players to do!

The Australian team in that second Test was Garry Jack [Balmain]; Kerry Boustead [Manly], Gene Miles [Wynnum-Manly], Mal Meninga [South's Brisbane], Eric Grothe [Parramatta]; Wally Lewis [Wynnum-Manly captain], Mark Murray [Redcliffe]; Dave Brown [Manly], Greg Conescu [Gladstone Brothers], Greg Dowling [Wynnum-Manly], Paul Vautin [Manly], Brian Niebling [Redcliffe] and Wayne Pearce [Balmain]. The two subs were Steve Mortimer [Canterbury-

Bankstown] and Wally Fullerton-Smith [Redcliffe]. The Great Britain side was Mick Burke [Widnes]; Des Drummond [Leigh], Garry Schofield [Hull FC], Keith Mumby [Bradford Northern], Ellery Hanley [Bradford Northern]; Tony Myler [Widnes], Neil Holding [St Helens]; Keith Rayne [Leeds], Brian Noble [Bradford Northern captain], Lee Crooks [Hull FC], Chris Burton [Hull Kingston Rovers], Andy Goodway [Oldham] and Mick Worrall [Oldham]. The subs were Andy Gregory [Widnes] and Mick Adams [Widnes]. The referee was once again Mr Shrimpton of New Zealand and the attendance was 26,534.

> With all the injuries, only half the quad were fit to play and losing the series one would think nothing else would happen to us. Forget it! We had a whole bunch of players go down with a 'flu virus. Fortunately the recovery was quick and most of the squad were over it before the final Test. Although the series was lost, I was determined that our side should play with the same resolution that they had shown throughout the tour and in that final Test they did not let me down.

Britain took the lead in this Test after Mal Meninga had given the Aussies an advantage with a penalty goal. Frank's men did not cross the half way line for 23 minutes but the first time they did they registered a fine try. Tony Myler produced a wonderful break to half way, a quick play the ball and Neil Holding fed Garry Schofield who immediately found Ellery Hanley tearing up in support. He bumped off two tacklers and raced 45 yards to the posts for Mick Burke to convert. Eight minutes later, Holding slotted over a neat drop goal. Unfortunately, that was the end of our scoring but the Aussies added to their tally with tries from Eric Grothe, Greg Conescu, and Garry Jack and Mal Maninga landed another three goals giving the Aussies a 20–7 win. For Australia, Steve Mortimer took over from Mark Murray at scrum half. Out went Dave Brown and Paul Vautin to be replaced by Brian Niebling and Wally Fullerton-Smith. Wayne Pearce moved up into the second row to give the great Ray Price his final appearance for Australia at loose forward. For Britain, Dave Hobbs [Featherstone

Rovers] came in at open side prop for Keith Rayne, who moved to sub forward and Brian Case [Wigan] came in for Lee Crooks at blind side prop, with Mick Adams taking over at loose forward from Mick Worrall. Mike Smith [Hull Kingston Rovers] was the sub back. The referee was another Kiwi, Mr A. Drake and the attendance was an expectedly low 18,756 and, of course, the game was played at the Sydney Cricket Ground.

Frank's final words on the Australian leg of the tour were that:

Although we lost the series, at no stage did our heads go down. Indeed in that final Test, up to half time we gave the all-conquering Aussies as good as we got. I was not happy with some of the decisions of either of the two New Zealanders who officiated in the three Tests but to be fair neither were the Aussies. We were constantly penalised for offside, and this did not help our cause. I spoke earlier about having experienced Test quality players if you were to make an impact in these Tests. The Australians had more than us, we knew that from the start but Grothe, Lewis, Pearce, Miles and Meninga shone whenever they played in these Test matches. They were frankly too good for us. Deep down I thought it would be so. Yes we failed, but we failed with honour. I was proud of the young men who fought so hard for their country. There was no surrender. Not all heroes are victorious and if you had seen the effort and the spirit of our men in all three Test matches, you would not sniff from the comfort of your armchair and say they were failures. It is impossible to give better than your utmost and that is what these players gave me and Great Britain.

The tour continued across the Tasman Sea with eight games in New Zealand, including three Test matches. There was also one final game in Papua New Guinea. In New Zealand, we came across a side which had been produced by the then director of coaching for the New Zealand rugby league, the late, former Wigan key stand off half, Ces Mountford. At this time, 1984, the Kiwis were almost equal to the Australians. I say almost, as the following year I saw all three Tests between the Aussies and the Kiwis and the New Zealanders could have, nay should have, won all three. In the final Test in that series the Kiwis won by something like 18–0, in the middle Test they were beaten by a John Ribot touchline conversion in injury time, after looking all over winners. In the first Test, I think the difference between the sides was, at most, three points. That is how good the Kiwis were at the time we played this Test series against them.

The warm up game was up in the far north of the North Island, in Whangarei against Northern Districts. Britain won the contest against a mostly Maori side by 42–8. The next game was the first Test at Carlaw Park, Auckland. Rain, rain and more rain made the playing area a morass. The Kiwi side had several of their 1980 tourists selected for this Test plus one or two new faces promoted to the side via the Ces Mountford coaching schools. Mud over the boot tops made for a forward battle, as little was expected to be seen of swift cross field handling in these conditions. The Kiwis selected a big, strong team, Garry Kemble [Hull FC]; Dean Bell [Auckland], James Leuluai [Hull FC], Fred Ah Kuoi [Hull FC captain], Dane O'Hara [Hull FC]; Olsen Filipaina [Balmain], Shane Varley [Auckland]; Kevin Tamati [Widnes], Howie Tamati [Taranaki], Dane Sorenson [Eastern Suburbs, Sydney], Kurt Sorenson [Eastern Suburbs, Sydney], Owen Wright [Auckland] and Hugh McGahan [Auckland]. The subs were Clayton Friend [Auckland] and Rickie Cowan [Auckland]. Great Britain selected from the fit players available Mick Burke [Widnes]; Des Drummond [Leigh], Garry Schofield [Hull FC], Keith Mumby [Bradford Northern], Ellery Hanley [Bradford Northern]; Mike Smith [Hull Kingston Rovers], Neil Holding [St Helens]; David Hobbs [Featherstone Rovers], Brian Noble [Bradford Northern, captain], Brian Case [Wigan], Chris Burton [Hull Kingston Rovers], Andy Goodway [Oldham] and Mick Adams [Widnes]. Andy Gregory [Widnes] and John Joyner [Castleford] were the subs.

The Kiwis scored the only two tries in this game. James Leuluai stepped through the mud for a good try after a great break by Kurt

Sorenson and a fantastic pass by the second rower. Then Howie Tamati put Fred Ah Kuoi in for Olsen Filipaino to convert the two, giving New Zealand the victory by 12–0. Australia provided two referees for these Tests and Mr Kevin Roberts, a Sydney policeman, officiated in the first before an attendance of 10,238.

Two games were played between the first and second Tests, New Zealand Maoris were beaten in Huntly 19–8 and Central Districts in Wellington were also beaten 38–6. Then the tourists travelled down to the South Island to Christchurch and after that were due to play the second Test. The venue was the Addington Show Grounds on 22 July. Again there was continuous drizzle throughout the 80 minutes of this game. The Kiwis maintained the same team which had won so well up in Auckland, but Britain had to make changes because of an injury to Garry Schofield, Ellery Hanley moving into the centre with Joe Lydon taking his place on the wing. Frank also changed the half backs bringing in the Widnes pair of Tony Myler at stand off and Andy Gregory at scrum half. The subs were John Joyner and Kevin Beardmore, both of Castleford. Once again the on form Kiwis totally dominated the game. Scoring five tries to two through Dean Bell, James Leuluai, Dane O'Hara (2) and Fred Ah Kuoi and four Olsen Filipaina goals to tries by Ellery Hanley and Tony Myler and two goals by Mick Burke, the Kiwis won the series and the game by 28–12. The referee was Mr B. Barnes and the attendance 3,824.

South Island were beaten by 36–14 again in Christchurch before the team headed north back to Auckland to play the final two games of the New Zealand section of the tour, the final Test and the traditional last game against Auckland. The third and final Test in New Zealand took the 1984 tourists to an unwelcome record as they became the first tourists to lose all the Tests played in a series in New Zealand and to extend their losing Test match sequence to six Tests. The Kiwis were ecstatic as the whistle sounded to end this series—they won the game 32–16—reaching the highest score by New Zealand in a Test match against Great Britain. Being in confident mood from the start of the series, and being able to field an unchanged side for all three Tests, New Zealand were worthy and deserved winners. Again they scored five tries to Britain's two, James Leuluai (2), Clayton Friend (2) and Dane O'Hara crossing for tries and Olsen Filipaina kicked six goals. Britain's reply was a try each to Ellery Hanley and Keith Mumby and four goals to Mick Burke. Mr Roberts was the referee and the attendance at Carlaw Park was 7,967.

The final game of this leg in New Zealand ended in an 18–16 defeat for Great Britain again at the hands of a spirited Auckland select side. There was another Test match to play before the troops came home and that was in Mount Hagen, Papua New Guinea. But Frank had seen his side give everything for little reward, as he reflected on leaving New Zealand:

Hard Test matches take their toll on players. Being close to the team you see how the physical effort of a hard tour drains them. Fit, young men appear to age so quickly in the course of a Test match. They leave the field with gaunt faces and this indicates the immense strain, physically and mentally, they have undergone. On the Australian leg of the tour our boys did wonderfully well to hold this excellent Australian side to the margins they did. It took a superhuman effort on their part. Our forwards, in the most, held the big Australian pack but the great players in their midfield and on the wings swung things their way. Once again I left Australia a disappointed man! For the second time I climbed on board a plane in Sydney feeling down hearted (I felt much the same in 1966). But I also remembered the feeling we all had in 1970. What helped me through this time was the knowledge that some time in the future another band of British players would be returning to Australia to resume the fight. As long as rugby league flourishes in our two countries, the Test series will be a war without end. And I hope this war continues forever.

The first Test match between Great Britain and Papua New Guinea was played at the Rebiamul Oval, Mount Hagen. Humidity played a big part in the Lions gradual fade out towards the end of the game. But before heat exhaustion set in, Great Britain set about their task in good style, running up a half time score of 22–4.

The ground, although small by British standards, was full to the rafters with thousands locked out. The Great Britain side was Mick Burke [Widnes, 1 try and 5 goals]; Des Drummond [Leigh, 2 tries], Ellery Hanley [Bradford Northern, 1 try], Keith Mumby [Bradford Northern, 1 try], Joe Lydon [Widnes]; Tony Myler [Widnes], Andy Gregory [Widnes]; Keith Rayne [Leeds, 1 try], Brian Noble [Bradford Northern, captain], Andy Goodway [Oldham], Terry Flanagan [Oldham], David Hobbs [Featherstone Rovers, 1 try] and Mick Adams [Widnes]. The subs were Steve Donlan [Leigh] and Wayne Proctor [Hull FC].

Papua New Guinea fielded M. Kitimun [Hawkes, Port Moresby]; N. Kania [Tarangau, Mount Hagen], D. Noifa [Paga Panthers, 1 try], B. Numapo [Brothers, Simbu, 2 goals], R. Tolik [Defence, Wewak, 1 try]; G. Gabob [Tarangau, Port Moresby], P. Kila [Tarangau, Port Moresby]; J. Tep [Brothers, Mount Hagen, captain], F. Asarufa [Magani, Kainantu], R. Jakis [Ela Country, Wewak, 1 try], R. Kubak [Brothers, Mount Hagen], R. Loitive [Defence, Port Moresby] and A. Taumaku [DCA, Port Moresby, 1 try]. The subs were J. Peter [Muruks, Rabaul] and P. Wek [Brothers, Mount Hagen]. The referee was the late Mr Barry Gomersall of Queensland and the official attendance was 7,510.

The 38–20 Great Britain win gave a great deal of pleasure to the local spectators, even though they lost, as just to see players from overseas was a real treat as rugby league is the National game of Papua New Guinea. So Frank and his team boarded the plane, returned home and another great adventure was over!

In the 1984–85 season Harvey Ashworth succeeded Ray Hatton as Chairman and I returned from the tour and assumed a new role as team manager of Oldham. Oldham finished fifth in the top division, their highest position since the 1950s. Only Hull KR, St Helens, Wigan and Leeds finished higher. During this season the bulk of our top players such as Alan McCurrie, Mike Taylor, Mick Morgan, Paddy Kirwan, Des Foy, Colin Hawkyard, Andy Goodway, Wally Jones, Green Vigo, Brian Caffery, Terry Flanagan, Mick Worrall and the Australian, Paul Taylor, had played 20 or more games, while Mick Parrish had played in all 35 games. During the season we had acquired Paul Taylor and Chris Phelan from Australia and we got David Hobbs from Featherstone on a £40,000 deal, but he was hurt early on.

At the end of this season I signed a contract with Oldham covering the 1985–86 and 1986–87 seasons. In doing so I became the first Oldham boss under contract since Griff Jenkins in 1973–74. Incidentally, this was the first contract I had signed in my long career as a coach!

We finished the 1985–86 season ninth with 30 points. Andy Goodway was sold to Wigan for £65,000 and we acquired brothers David and Glen Liddiard, Mal Graham, Gary Warnecke and David Topliss. The highlight of the season was the run up to the Challenge Cup semi final. David Topliss was injured in a car crash in Wakefield in January 1986 and he was badly missed over the second half of the season. Despite that, we got to the semi final of the cup with wins against Carlisle at Boundary Park and against Warrington and Bradford at Watersheddings.

The team on that day was David Liddiard; Hussein M'Barki, Des Foy, Gary Warnecke, Mike Taylor; Glen Liddiard, Ray Ashton; Wally Jones, Ian Sanderson, David Hobbs, Mick Worrall, Mal Graham and Terry Flanagan, with Mick Parrish and Tom Nadiola replacing the injured Glen Liddiard and Terry Flanagan at half time. This was probably the best team Oldham had had while I had been in charge.

We lost the semi final 18–7 to Castleford. At half time the score was 7–7. Bob Beardmore scored twice for Castleford but one of his tries was controversial. The Beardmore try, that put Castleford ahead, was contentious because he put the ball down over the try line but one of his feet was over the dead ball line! Television replays proved this to have been the case.

The 1986–87 season was our fifth consecutive year in the top flight, but it was a strange season with lots of highlights yet still ended in relegation. Early on we reached the Lancashire Cup Final with wins over Leigh, Workington and Widnes before losing 27–6 to Wigan in the final at Knowsley Road. Then came that magnificent performance against the Australians at Watersheddings when we lost only 22–16. The team on that day was: Jeff Edwards; Paul Sherman, Des Foy, Gary Warnecke, Hussein M'Barki; David Topliss, Ray Ashton; Bruce Clark, Terry Flanagan, Neil Clawson, Mick Worrall, David Hobbs, Stuart Raper, subs: Colin Hawkyard and Tom Nadiole.

There was still better to come when, in February we beat mighty Wigan 10–8 at Watersheddings with the Kirwan try and the Mick Burke goal to win the game. The Oldham team for that game was: Mick Burke; Hussein M'barki, Des Foy, Gary Bridge, Mike Taylor; David Topliss, Paddy Kirwan; Bruce Clark, Ian Sanderson, Hugh Waddell, Mick Worrall, David Hobbs, Terry Flanagan, subs: Gary Warnecke and Stuart Raper. They were two of the best and most exciting games seen at Watersheddings in the last 50 years, yet we still ended up relegated.

Having completed five seasons with Oldham I decided to call it a day and resigned. My thoughts at the time were very sad as I had thoroughly enjoyed my stay there and had met lots of nice people. During my time at the club the Chairman Ray Hatton, and his successor Harvey Ashworth and the directors had always backed me 100 per cent. Harvey Ashworth in particular was always very supportive. He was a long standing supporter and director of the club and I knew, from the many conversations I had with him, that it was always his dream for Oldham to go to Wembley. I would really like to make a special mention of everyone at Oldham who helped to make my time at the club so enjoyable, but there were so many that it would be impossible to mention them all by name. From the directors, coaching staff and players, down to the great fans who supported us, the list would be far too long. However, I would like to put on record my appreciation to all those who helped and supported me during my time at the club. My resignation was amicably received and I left Oldham with sadness but happy in the knowledge that I had made some great and lasting friendships.

Frank's position as coach of Great Britain ended an epic international rugby league career and although his 1970 Ashes victory was his most memorable win, he made a consistently outstanding contribution in any international and club game he was involved in, whether it be as a player or coach. After his return from the Australia Tour in 1984, it was impossible for Frank not be involved in rugby league. As Frank said earlier, when your life is as thoroughly embroiled in rugby league as his, it's difficult not to be involved in the game at some level.

So Frank found himself back in the saddle at Widnes briefly during the 1991–92 season and during that stay the club won the Regal Trophy. He continued on after that as club secretary until his retirement in December 2003.

Overall Frank was a fantastic rugby league player: his adaptability and toughness on the pitch were key components to his success, and his infamous Widnes sense of humour helped as well. He played a remarkable 365 games for Widnes, 139 games for Saints and 48 games for Rochdale Hornets. Add to this his 20 games for Lancashire and his 24 games for Great Britain and it's easy to see that Frank had an amazing playing career spanning 19 years. He and Eileen were blessed with four children, Greg, Denise, Chris and Helen who have between them given Eileen and Frank seven grandchildren, Chris, Danny, Liam, Sean, Megan, Sonny and Frankie. In July 2004 Frank was made an Honorary Freeman of the Borough of Halton. This was an especially personal gift and Frank says, 'that despite all the honours received within the game, being made a Freeman of my home town is something I cherish above everything else. I am extremely grateful to the people of Widnes for bestowing this honour on me'. He also makes special mention of the Widnes club and supporters to whom he gives his thanks and expresses the hope that Widnes Vikings will return to Super League where they belong. As this biography concludes, Frank still enjoys his golf at the Widnes Golf Club and loves to talk about the game that provided so many great memories for both him and rugby league fans.

APPENDIX

Frank's Club Playing Record

Widnes
Debut 27 December 1955 v Liverpool City [H] 2 tries.
Final game 25 August 1967 v Halifax [A].

	A	T	G
1955–56	15	7	0
1956–57	20	5	0
1957–58	40	22	0
1958–59	38	34	0
1959–60	41	18	1
1960–61	26	7	0
1961–62	29	11	1
1962–63	37	12	2
1963–64	41	7	0
1964–65	26 +1	3	1
1965–66	21+ 1	10	0
1966–67	28	9	2
1967–68	3	1	0
Totals	**365 +2**	**146**	**7**

St Helens
Debut 1 September 1967 v Salford [H].
Final game 13 March 1971 v Hull KR [A].

	A	T	G
1967–68	29	10	0
1968–69	44	15	0
1969–70	44	16	2
1970–71	22 + 5	5	0
Totals	**139 + 5**	**46**	**2**

Rochdale Hornets

Debut 7 August 1971 v Barrow [A] Lancashire Cup.

Final game 7 January 1973 v Salford [H].

	A	**T**	**G**
1971–72	32 +1	10	0
1972–73	16 +1	8	0
Totals	**48 +2**	**18**	**0**

Frank's County Playing Record

Lancashire * As Captain.

Debut 31 August 1959.

Last game 11 November 1970.

31–8–59 v Cumberland at Workington L 8–14

11–11–59 v Yorkshire at Leigh L 28–38 3 tries

31–8–60 v Yorkshire at Wakefield W 21–20

27–5–61 v Cumberland at Salford W 32–18 1 try

13–9–61 v New Zealand at Warrington W 15–13

9–10–61 v Yorkshire at Leigh W 14–12 1 try

12–9–62 v Cumberland at Widnes W 28–8 1 try

26–9–62 v Yorkshire at Wakefield L 8- 22

11–9–63 v Yorkshire at St Helens W 45–20

25–9–63 v Australia at Wigan W 13–11

2–10–63 v Cumberland at Whitehaven L 8–13

20–9–65 v Cumberland at Whitehaven L 11–14

13–10–65 v New Zealand at St Helens L 10–21

21–9–66 v Yorkshire at Leeds W 22–17

12–10–66 v Cumberland at Warrington L14–18

12–9–67 v Cumberland* at Workington W 19–6 1try

11–10–67 v Australia* at Salford L 2–14

24–1–68 v Yorkshire at Widnes W 23–17

24–8–69 v Cumberland at Workington W 30–10

11–11–70 v Cumberland* at Barrow W 28–5 2 tries

Totals 20 games [3 as captain] 9 tries

Frank's International Playing Record

England
Debut 17 November 1962.
17–11–62 v France at Leeds, W 18–6.
Total 1 game

Great Britain   * As Captain
Debut 24 September 1960
Last game 7 November 1970
24–9–60 v New Zealand in World Cup at Bradford, W 23–8 1 try
1–10–60 v France in World Cup at Swinton, W 33–7 1 try
8–10–60 v Australia in World Cup at Bradford W 10–3
11–12–60 v France in Bordeaux W 21–10 1 try
28–1–61 v France at St Helens W 27–8
2–12–62 v France in Perpignan L 12–17
9–11–63 v Australia at Swinton L 12–50
6–12–64 v France in Perpignan L 8–18
23–1–65 v France at Swinton W 17–7
25–9–65 v New Zealand at Swinton W 7–2
16–7–66 v Australia ['66 tour] in Brisbane L 4–6
6–8–66 v New Zealand ['66 tour] in Auckland W 25–8 1 try,
        sub for Hardisty
20–8–66 v New Zealand ['66 tour] in Auckland W 22–14
22–1–67 v France in Carcassonne W 16–13
4–3–67 v France at Wigan L 13–23
6–6–70 v Australia* ['70 tour] in Brisbane L 15–37
20–6–70 v Australia* ['70 tour] in Sydney W 28–7
4–7–70 v Australia* ['70 tour] in Sydney W 21–17
11–7–70 v New Zealand* ['70 tour] in Auckland W 19–15
19–7–70 v New Zealand* ['70 tour] in Christchurch W 23–9 1 try
25–7–70 v New Zealand* ['70 tour] in Auckland W 33–16
24–10–70 v Australia* [World Cup] at Leeds W 11–4
28–10–70 v France* [World Cup] at Castleford W 6–0
7–11–70 v Australia* [World Cup Final] at Leeds L 7–12
Totals 24 games [9 as captain] 5 tries